VEGAN ROMANIA

Mihaela Lica Butler

Cover design: Maria Patricia K. Revita
Author photographs: Angela Schmitt
Editor: Laura Spencer (www.writingthoughts.com)

ISBN: 1519790902
ISBN-13: 978-1519790903

To my grandmother, Victoria Gheţe, who inspired my love for cooking.

Contents

ROMANIAN VEGAN CUISINE

Romania is little known for its vegan cuisine. In fact, Romanians enjoy meats more than anything else. Their traditional foods are usually rich in fats and spices. But in the countryside, people cannot always afford meat. They substitute animal fats with a wide variety of vegan dishes instead. Vegan food is also enjoyed in all its diversity during several fasting seasons, especially during the 40 days of Lent.

I have collected these recipes from my travels around Romania, as well as from my relatives, and especially from my grandmother, who lived in the south of the country, in Teleorman County, in the historical region of Muntenia.

Every recipe featured in this bundle is tried, tested, or adapted by me to suit a healthy vegan, or vegetarian diet.

To cook like a Romanian, always have the following spices in your home: onion, garlic, salt and pepper, paprika powder, loads of parsley, dill, and lovage (leuștean). By the way, there's never enough garlic. Feel free to add more to every recipe!

I usually freeze parsley, dill and lovage in batches, but I prefer fresh herbs when in season. Try to avoid dried herbs, because they are slower to release their flavors than fresh herbs. If you cannot find fresh, soak dried herbs overnight covered in oil to release their flavors.

Many of the dishes in the first chapter (Appetizers and Salads) are intended to be served along with other dishes, but some can also be served as main meals. It is up to you how you create your menus.

Appetizers and Salads

1. Zucchini Fritters

This delicious zucchini dish is an excellent vegan snack from spring to late summer. Fritters can be used in main dishes too. Serve with garlic dip, vegan sauce, or any other way you see fit.

- 4 zucchinis
- 1 large onion, finely chopped
- 2 garlic cloves, finely crushed
- 1 bunch fresh parsley, finely chopped
- Salt and pepper to taste
- 2 tablespoons olive oil
- Breadcrumbs for breading
- Oil for frying (preferably canola oil)

- ❖ Wash the zucchinis, then grate them over the large holes of the vegetable grater.
- ❖ Squeeze the liquid out to drain the zucchinis using a clean dishcloth.
- ❖ Mix well with olive oil, onion, garlic and parsley. Season with salt and pepper to taste and stir well.
- ❖ Form patties with your hands, roll in breadcrumbs, then fry in hot oil for a couple of minutes on each side until golden. Drain the excess fat on paper towels, then serve warm.

Serving ideas: over pasta with mushroom sauce; with garlic dip; with avocado and cucumber dip; with fresh salad; as snack at parties.

2. Potato Fritters: Base Recipe

Potato fritters are often found in Romanian restaurants served as a side dish, but they are traditionally made with egg. I have adapted the traditional recipe to create a vegan version.

- 7 medium large potatoes
- 1 large carrot
- ½ knob celery
- 1 red onion, finely chopped
- 2 garlic cloves, finely chopped
- 1 bunch fresh dill, finely chopped
- Salt and pepper to taste
- 2 tablespoons olive oil
- Water to boil
- Breadcrumbs
- Canola oil for frying

- ❖ Wash and peel the vegetables, then place into a large pot with water. Allow to boil until softened.
- ❖ Mash the vegetables, then mix well with olive oil, onion, garlic and dill. Season with salt and pepper to taste. Mix well.
- ❖ Form patties with your hands, roll in breadcrumbs, then fry in hot oil for a couple of minutes on each side until golden. Drain the excess fat on paper towels, then serve warm.

Serving ideas: as snack at parties, with a dip of your choice; as a side dish for main dishes.

Variation: Bake the patties instead of frying them. Cook for about 25-30 minutes at 180°C (or until golden brown).

- Potato Fritters Variation 1: Parsnip and Thyme

Take the base recipe and replace the knob celery with two parsnips. Instead of fresh dill, use fresh thyme, finely chopped. Prepare as instructed above.

- Potato Fritters Variation 2: Root Parsley and Mixed Herbs

Replace the ½ knob celery in the base recipe with 2 parsley roots. Instead of fresh dill, use a combination of chives, lovage, and coriander. Prepare as instructed.

3. Lentil Paste: Base Recipe

This special paste is a beautiful bread spread. It can be kept in the fridge for up to one week. It is adapted from the traditional lentil main dish, a staple in many Romanian homes.

- 1 cup lentils (200 grams)
- 3 cups water
- 1 bay leaf
- 1 red onion, finely chopped
- 3 garlic cloves, finely chopped
- 1 bunch fresh parsley, finely chopped
- 2 tablespoons olive oil
- 1 teaspoon sweet paprika powder
- Salt and pepper to taste

- ❖ Wash the lentils well, then bring to a boil with the 3 cups of water and the bay leaf. Heat over medium heat, for about 30-35 minutes.
- ❖ In a separate frying pan, sauté the onion and garlic in oil with paprika powder until soft, for about 10 minutes.
- ❖ When the lentils have boiled remove the bay leaf. Pour them into a food processor. Add the sautéed garlic and onion. Add salt and pepper, then parsley. Blitz the mixture for about 2 minutes, until creamy. Taste for salt, and add as much as you need.

Serving ideas: on bread, or pita, as a creamy base for main dishes, with pasta and so on.

- Lentil Paste Variation 1: Mushrooms

To the base recipe, add 450 grams of canned wild mushrooms. Sauté them with the garlic and onion for about 30 minutes. Blend in the food processor with the lentils for about four minutes, until you obtain a homogenous paste.

- Lentil Paste Variation 2: Tomato

Replace the paprika powder in the base recipe with 4 fresh tomatoes, chopped coarsely. Then, prepare as instructed. Don't overcook the tomatoes since you want them to keep their natural flavors and the vitamins.

4. Zucchini Paste

This special paste, or **pâté**, can be served as a spread or as a dip. Traditionally, it is consumed for breakfast or during Lent (when it is cooked without oil).

- 1 zucchini
- 2 tablespoons olive oil
- 1 large onion
- 2 garlic cloves

- 1/2 teaspoons lemon juice
- Fresh parsley to garnish (optional)
- Salt and pepper to taste

- ❖ Peel the zucchini and cut it into small cubes.
- ❖ Peel the onion and slice it into rings.
- ❖ Peel the garlic and chop it finely.
- ❖ Heat oil in a pan, then add the onion and zucchini. Sauté on medium heat until soft, about 10 minutes.
- ❖ Allow to cool a few minutes, then put in a bowl with lemon juice, garlic, salt and pepper to taste.
- ❖ Mix to achieve a homogeneous consistency.

Serving ideas: on bread, or pita, as dip, with pasta and so on. When you serve it as a dip, place it in a soup bowl and garnish with fresh parsley and fresh sliced tomatoes.

5. Mushroom Paste

A beautiful, tasty dish, easy to prepare, and pretty basic. You can always get creative to make it more interesting.

- 300 g fresh mushrooms
- 2 onions
- 2 slices French bread

- 4 tablespoons olive oil
- Salt and pepper to taste

- ❖ Wash the mushrooms well, then cut them in halves. Boil in salted water for 15-20 minutes.
- ❖ After boiling drain through a sieve, but don't discard the stock. Use it to soak the bread in.
- ❖ Soak the bread, then squeeze.
- ❖ Grate the onion and sauté in oil with mushrooms, salt and pepper until slightly golden.
- ❖ Allow to cool completely, then puree with a mixer, until you obtain a homogeneous pâté.
- ❖ Season, as needed, with more salt and pepper.
- ❖ Allow the mixture to cool in the fridge for at least one hour before you serve it.

Serving ideas: on bread, or on pita: this is a spread. You can always season with herbs and garlic for that extra zing.

6. Mushroom and Potato Cutlets

This dish replaces the famous pan-fried minced meat croquettes, which are traditional in Romania and are called "chiftelute."

- 4 large potatoes, cooked
- 2 small onions, grated
- 300 gr fresh mushrooms
- 1 bunch fresh parsley, finely chopped
- 3 tablespoons flour
- 3 tablespoons breadcrumbs
- Fresh rosemary and thyme, chopped
- Salt and pepper to taste
- Olive oil – enough for frying the cutlets

- ❖ Wash the mushrooms well, then cut them in halves. Boil in salted water for 15-20 minutes.
- ❖ After boiling drain through a sieve, then chop finely.
- ❖ Mash the boiled potatoes in a bowl, then add the mushrooms, chopped parsley, grated onion, breadcrumbs, flour, salt and pepper. Mix until homogeneous.
- ❖ Dust your hands with flour to help you form the patties, which should be fried in hot oil for about three minutes on each side until crispy. Drain on kitchen paper to remove excess fat.

Serving ideas: with a nice tomato and garlic dip. They can also be the base for a main dish when served with generous vegan sides.

7. Mashed Beans: Base Recipe

This recipe is the basis for the famous "fasole bătută" – another Romanian cuisine staple. There are many variations of the dish – the base recipe serves as a good starting point.

- 500 gr dried beans
- 3 garlic cloves
- 2 large onions, cut julienne
- 1 tsp. paprika

- 3 bay leaves (dry)
- 4 tbsp. olive oil
- Salt and pepper to taste

- ❖ Soak the beans in water for about 6 hours before cooking them. Soaking them too long (as in overnight) may cause them to ferment, which destroys their flavor.
- ❖ In a large pot place one part beans and three parts water. Add the bay leaves, then bring gently to boil. Cook until the beans are nice and soft (for about 1 hour, but it could take longer depending on the variety of beans that you use. Romanians typically use Phaseolus vulgaris, the common bean.).
- ❖ Strain through a sieve, but don't discard the water – it will make a valuable stock later on.
- ❖ Use a mixer to mash the beans together with the garlic cloves, salt and pepper.
- ❖ In a frying pan, sauté the onions in olive oil until golden and season with paprika. Remove them from the pan, but do not discard the oil.
- ❖ Add the mashed beans to the pan and reduce heat to minimum. Stir until the oil is homogenously incorporated into the bean mash. If the consistency of the paste is too thick, add some of the bean stock until you achieve a better result. The end paste should still be thick, but not hard.
- ❖ Place into a deep serving bowl and pour the onions on top.

Serving ideas: with a nice sauerkraut salad; with pickles, as a side dish; or as a main dish on bread or on pita. It also works nicely on toast.

- Mashed Beans Variation 1: Fresh Tomato and Garlic

Take the base recipe and enhance with freshly chopped tomatoes and garlic. Spread on bread, like a bruschetta. Oh, so delicious!

- Mashed Beans Variation 2: Fresh Mushrooms

This is really not customary, but it's to die for. Add freshly chopped mushrooms to your beans for the extra flavor that makes the difference.

You can always make this dish yours by improving it with whatever fresh ingredient you fancy. Still, remember that the Romanian original is a pretty basic dish (to be honest, it does not need much else to be unforgettable!) Poftă bună! (Bon Appetite!)

8. Carrot and White Beans Paste

This is something easy and light, perfect as a light snack. It is a base recipe that can be improved with other root vegetables, such as parsnips and root parsley. My grandmother usually rescued the roots from the vegetable stock to prepare this.

- 2 boiled carrots
- 1 cup white beans (boiled)
- 2 tbsp. olive oil

- 1 garlic clove
- Salt and pepper to taste

❖ Put all the ingredients in a food processor and puree until smooth

Serving ideas: on toast, garnished with fresh parsley, or fresh spring onion, or on salted crackers.

9. Mushrooms Stuffed with Fried Onion

This is something you will find in several international cuisines, in many variations. The Romanian recipe is pretty basic, very easy to make – requiring virtually no cookery skills. It is a staple during the 40 days of Lent (when it is cooked without oil – you would sauté the ingredients in a bit of water).

- 20 large white mushrooms, stemmed (don't discard the stems)
- 20 mushroom stems, minced
- 1 garlic clove, peeled and minced
- 2 large onions, peeled and minced coarsely
- 2 tbsp. canola oil
- Fresh parsley (to garnish)
- Salt and pepper to taste
- Juice from ½ lemon

- ❖ Preheat the oven at 200°C/400°F. Wash your mushrooms. Pat them dry with kitchen towels. Set them on a large baking tray cavity side up and then coat them with lemon juice. Set aside.
- ❖ In a frying pan preheat the oil. Turn the heat to medium-low. Tip in the garlic, onions and stems. Stir fry for about 10 minutes, until the onion becomes golden. Season with salt and pepper to taste.
- ❖ Using a teaspoon, fill the lemon-coated mushrooms with the onion-garlic-mushroom composition.
- ❖ Bake until the mushrooms are tender and the filling is heated through and golden on top, about 25 minutes.

Serving ideas: on toast, garnished with fresh parsley, or fresh spring onion, or on salted crackers.

10.   Grilled Mushrooms Stuffed with Fresh Tomato Salad

This is not a widespread dish, but it makes for a delicious cold appetizer. It was something we enjoyed during the summer months in Crângeni, Teleorman.

- 20 large white mushrooms, stemmed
- 2 large tomatoes (or more, depending on the size of your mushrooms)
- 3 spring onions, minced
- 1 tbsp. sunflower oil
- Fresh parsley (to garnish)
- Salt to taste

- ❖ Fire up your grill (an electric grill will do, too).
- ❖ Wash your mushrooms and pat them dry with kitchen towels. Place them on the grill, first cavity-side down (we do not need the juices for this particular dish), then shortly on the other side.
- ❖ Remove mushrooms from the grill. Set them aside on kitchen towels, cavity-side down, to absorb the excess juices.
- ❖ Deseed and peel your tomatoes, then chop them into small cubes.
- ❖ Mix with diced onions and oil.
- ❖ Season with salt to taste.
- ❖ Fill the grilled mushrooms with this fresh tomato salad and set in the fridge to chill for 30 minutes before serving.
- ❖ Garnish with fresh parsley.

Serving ideas: on a leaf of lettuce, on a nice green salad bed, on toast, or with other cold starters.

11.   Eggplant and Tomato Salad

Romanians love their eggplant salad, which is usually very similar to baba ganoush (eggplant casserole). However, this salad counts on steamed or boiled eggplant. It is easier to prepare and it tastes delicious.

- 1 large eggplant
- 1 large onion, julienne
- 2 large tomatoes, cubed

- 1 bunch flat leaf parsley, chopped
- 1tbsp. olive oil
- Salt and pepper to taste

- ❖ Peel the eggplant. Cut it into cubes and immerse it into cold salted water for about 30 minutes. Pat dry on kitchen towels. Steam for 15-20 minutes. Alternatively, if you don't have a steamer, you can boil it until soft – 8-15 minutes, using 2 parts water to 1 part eggplant cubes. Remove from heat and discard the liquid through a sieve.
- ❖ In a large frying pan, preheat the oil and turn the heat to medium-low. Tip in the onion. Fry until golden before adding the tomatoes, parsley and eggplant. Cook about 20 minutes. Season with salt and pepper.

Serving ideas: this is a dish that can be enjoyed cold or warm. It tastes delicious on fresh homemade bread. You can enhance it with freshly roasted sesame seeds.

12.   Cauliflower Spread

Cauliflower is such a versatile vegetable. You will find it in many Romanian recipes, especially in stews. This dish is fast and easy to prepare, the perfect breakfast spread.

- 1 cauliflower head, halved crosswise and sliced
- 2 garlic cloves, minced
- 1 spring onion, cut julienne
- 1tbsp. olive oil
- Salt and pepper to taste

- ❖ Boil the cauliflower in salty water, until soft – about 20 minutes. When ready, discard the water through a sieve and let cool off.
- ❖ Mash the cauliflower with a fork, then mix in the garlic and the oil. Season with salt and pepper. Served sprinkled with spring onions or with chives.

Serving ideas: this is typically a breakfast spread, but it can work for every occasion.

13. Tomato and Garlic Dip

For this lovely, summery dip all you need is a food processor and three fresh ingredients: tomato, celery, and garlic. Add some salt and pepper to taste, a drizzle of olive oil, and puree until foamy smooth. Perfection.

- 1 large tomato, cubed
- 1 celery stalk, chopped
- 1 garlic clove, minced

- 3 tbsp. olive oil
- Salt and pepper to taste

- ❖ Put all the ingredients into a food processor and puree until smooth. Chill well before serving.

Serving ideas: this is typically a dip, but it can also be used as salad dressing.

14.   Winter Root Vegetable Salad

"The health bomb," as some grandmas call it, this salad is filling, delicious and nutritious. It keeps you skinny, too!

- 1 knob celery
- 2 carrots
- 1 parsnip
- 1 root parsley

- 2 tbsp. olive oil
- Salt and pepper to taste
- Zest and juice from $\frac{1}{2}$ lemon

- ❖ Grate all root veggies on the side of the grater that has the smallest holes. Then mix in olive oil and the zest and juice from $\frac{1}{2}$ lemon. Season with salt to taste.

Although it sounds easy to make, the salad requires some of your time if you don't have electronic kitchen aids to grate the vegetable roots in a flash. You can serve this as a main dish or as a side dish. For example, serve with grilled or stuffed eggplant.

15.   Winter Potato Salad

This is one of the easiest recipes you'll ever need, simply delicious if you love potatoes. Although it is usually consumed in the winter, it may also be a Lent favorite (remember, do not use oil for Lent recipes). This is a monastery recipe from the historic region of Moldavia, Romania.

- 6-7 large potatoes, washed (leave the skin on)
- 1 large onion, finely minced
- 1 tbsp. tomato paste
- 2 tbsp. sunflower oil (alternatively olive oil or canola oil)
- Salt and pepper to taste

- ❖ Turn the burner on high and bring salted water to a boil. Put the potatoes in. Reduce the heat to medium. Allow to boil 30 minutes, all until the potatoes are tender all the way through.
- ❖ Remove the potatoes from heat, drain through a sieve, and allow them to cool off before peeling them.
- ❖ Grate the potatoes, or cut them into very small cubes.
- ❖ Put the potatoes in a large salad bowl. Add oil, onion, tomato paste, and season with salt and pepper to taste. Mix well.

The salad can be enjoyed on its own, or as a side dish for your vegan main dishes.

16.   Beetroot Salad

Another winter favorite, this beetroot salad is traditionally consumed in monasteries, mostly in the historic region of Moldavia, Romania. Variations, however, exist all over the country.

- 6 medium beets (washed, skins on)
- 3 garlic cloves, peeled and minced finely

- 2 tbsp. oil (olive oil, sunflower oil, or canola oil)
- ½ tsp. sugar
- Salt and pepper to taste

- ❖ Place water into a deep skillet and bring to a boil. Reduce heat to medium, add the beets and let simmer for about 45 minutes, until tender.
- ❖ Remove from heat and allow the beets to cool off before peeling them.
- ❖ Grate the beets on the coarser side of the grater.
- ❖ Place all the ingredients into a deep salad bowl and mix well.

Ideally, you will allow this salad to rest for at least 30 minutes before serving, but you can also consume it immediately. Some recipes call for a few drops of vinegar; others do not use sugar. It's up to you to make this recipe yours. Sprinkle with fresh parsley before serving: it gives the salad a vibrant contrast of colors. If you cook it for Lent, do not add oil.

17.   Red Cabbage Slaw

Red Cabbage, or purple cabbage as it is also known, is a wonderful vegetable, full of vitamin C and rich in vitamin A (it has ten times more vitamin A than green cabbage). This slaw is an Autumn/Winter favorite in Romania. Variations exist.

- 1 small red cabbage
- 2 carrots
- 1 apple
- 2-3 mandarin oranges (optional)

- 2 tbsp. olive oil
- 2 tbsp. lemon juice
- Zest from 1 lemon
- Salt and pepper to taste

- ❖ Grate the apple and carrots finely, then shred the cabbage as thinly as possible (or cut it julienne).
- ❖ Mix all the vegetables and apple in a large bowl, season with olive oil, zest and lemon juice, and add salt and pepper to your own taste. When done, mix in mandarin orange slices.

Like most Romanian salads, this can be enjoyed as a main dish, or as a side dish. It has a beautiful color and fine citrus aromas making it perfect for meals around Christmas time.

18.   Summer Peasant's Salad

This simple salad is based on the staples of the Romanian summer: ripe tomatoes, cucumbers and bell peppers. It's a happy, healthy dish, which can be enhanced with feta cheese if you are not a vegan.

- 1 cucumber, peeled and cubed
- 2 large tomatoes, cubed
- 1 bell pepper (any color would do), deseeded and cubed
- 1 large onion, cut julienne
- 1tbsp. olive oil
- 1 tbsp. wine vinegar
- Salt and pepper to taste

- ❖ Mix all the ingredients well in a large salad bowl. Refrigerate for 30 minutes before serving.

You can always add other ingredients to your salad to make it more interesting: boiled egg and feta cheese if you are not a vegan, or olives and fresh parsley. Occasionally, Romanians prepare this salad with garlic. Yes... there's never enough garlic!

19.   Fried Assorted Pickles

This recipe only works if you can get your hands on old-fashioned salt brine pickles. If you have a Romanian grocery store where you live, ask and they'll probably have a jar. Do not use vinegar pickles for this recipe. Pickles could be too salty for this dish – so keep them in water for an hour or so before use.

- As many assorted pickles as you want to fry: green tomatoes, cabbage leaves, peppers, etc. Slice some of the larger ones. Pat dry with kitchen towels.
- Oil for frying – usually sunflower oil.

❖   Heat 5-6 tablespoons of oil in a deep frying pan. Place the pickles in, and fry on both sides until golden. Do not overcrowd the pan: work in batches if necessary. Be careful when you fry pickles: some may be still full of juices and will cause the oil to splash. To be safe, squeeze the pickles dry before frying.

Serving ideas: the fried pickles can be mixed to make a salad, or can be consumed as they are, warm or cold, with your main dish.

20.   Traditional Roasted Eggplant Salad

Many Romanians roast the eggplants for this recipe in the oven. Traditionally, eggplants are charred over a flame (typically when firing the wood grill) for 15-30 minutes. Roasting on an open flame gives the flesh a delicate smoky flavor.

- 2 large eggplants
- 1 red onion, peeled and minced

- 2 tbsp. olive oil (or, traditionally, sunflower oil)
- Salt and pepper to taste
- Juice from ½ lemon

- ❖ Roast the eggplants in their skin as long as you need to until soft and the skin is charred. Turn a few times for even roasting. In the oven you would typically roast at 200°C, 400°F.
- ❖ When done, peel the eggplants and set to strain. Allow the juices to drain naturally, for about 20 minutes.
- ❖ Chop the eggplants with a wooden spoon until you reach the consistency of a paste. Pour into a salad bowl. Add onion, oil and lemon, and stir vigorously to incorporate well.
- ❖ Season with salt and pepper to your taste. Refrigerate for 30 minutes before serving.

Serving ideas: as a dip, on toast, with pita, stuffed in fresh tomatoes. Garnish with fresh parsley.

21.   Scalded Lettuce Salad

This is one of the easiest recipes to remember that I know. I call it the "rule of 2" because all ingredients come in pairs. It is also extremely easy to prepare, and very tasty.

- 2 lettuce heads, washed and torn
- 2 garlic cloves, minced
- 2 tbsp. olive oil (or, traditionally, sunflower oil)
- 2 tsp. lemon juice
- Salt and pepper to taste

- ❖ Heat a bit of water (3-4 tbsp.), with oil, garlic, and salt and pepper to taste.
- ❖ Tip in the torn lettuce, and toss gently.
- ❖ Drizzle lemon juice, toss and serve.

This is typically a side dish. Variations of the recipe exist - for example, you can boil the lettuce with everything else from the start. This, in my experience, destroys the vibrant color of the leafy green and makes lettuce too chewy. I prefer crispy lettuce, but you can try the boiling variant too. Don't keep the lettuce in the boiling liquid for more than a minute. Discard unwanted liquid through a sieve.

22.   Dandelion Green Salad

Ah, the stuff of gourmet eateries anywhere else, but in Romania this is something we'd call the poor folks' meal--easy to prepare, tasty and rich in minerals. Oh, and that dill does wonders to this dish.

- 1 kg dandelion greens
- 3 young garlics, with tender green leaves
- 2 tbsp. sunflower oil

- 1 bunch fresh dill, minced
- 1 tsp. vinegar (or 2 tsp. lemon juice)
- Salt and pepper to taste

- ❖ Wash, trim and roughly chop the dandelion greens. Repeat the action with the green young garlic.
- ❖ Place all ingredients into a deep salad bowl and toss gently a few times, until oil, vinegar and salt cover the greens evenly.

Serving ideas: on its own; as a salad bed for grilled mushrooms; as a side dish for a vegan main dish... or for every main dish you consider fit.

23. Sorrel Salad

The perfect little salad for early spring, this sorrel dish is probably the easiest thing in the world to prepare. It's not necessarily exclusive to Romanian cuisine (not many things are, as the world is a melting pot of traditions), but it is traditional and needed to be mentioned.

- 1 kg sorrel
- 3 tbsp. canola oil
- 1 tbsp. lemon juice
- Salt to taste

- ❖ Wash, trim and roughly chop your sorrel. Pat dry with kitchen towels.
- ❖ Place all ingredients into a deep salad bowl and toss gently a few times, until oil, lemon and salt cover the greens evenly.

Serving ideas: serve pretty much the same way you would serve dandelion green salad, or an ordinary, simple, lettuce salad. For everything else... use your imagination. You cannot go wrong when you love vegan food.

24.   Young Spinach Salad

Another exceptional spring companion, the spinach salad is too easy to prepare to miss. This one, however, calls for fresh garden herbs to become the favorite I remember. Have your fresh dill and flat parsley leaves ready!

- 1 kg baby spinach, washed, trimmed and roughly chopped
- 4 tbsp. freshly chopped dill
- 2 tbsp. freshly chopped parsley leaves

- 4 tbsp. olive oil
- 2 tbsp. lemon (or 1 tbsp. vinegar)
- Salt to taste

- ❖   Place all ingredients into a deep salad bowl and toss gently a few times until oil, lemon and salt cover the greens evenly.

25.   Simple Cucumber Salad

A refreshing summer recipe, perfect for hot days, this is one of my childhood favorites. It is important for you to follow this very easy recipe carefully if you want the authentic taste.

- 2 large cucumbers
- 1 tbsp. freshly chopped dill
- 2 garlic cloves, peeled and minced

- 1 tsp. sunflower oil
- 1 tbsp. vinegar
- Salt to taste

- ❖ Immerse the cucumbers into a bowl with icy water for 1 hour before making this salad.
- ❖ Peel cucumbers and slice lengthwise to remove the seeds.
- ❖ Cut cucumbers into thin slices, sprinkle with salt (toss gently to allow the salt to cover them evenly), then place the cucumbers to drain into a sieve.
- ❖ Place drained cucumbers into a deep salad bowl and toss gently with oil, vinegar, dill and garlic. Taste for salt and season as needed.

26.   Summer Salad

The clue is in the name: this simple, delicious salad captures the best of summer in just a few bites. As usual... there's never enough parsley!

- 5 tomatoes, sliced
- 5 garden cucumbers (small varieties), thinly sliced
- 1 lettuce head, chopped coarsely
- 2 pimiento peppers, trimmed, deseeded and chopped
- 1 bunch dill, chopped

- 1 bunch parsley, chopped
- 2 tbsp. vegetable oil
- 1 tbsp. lemon juice or vinegar
- 1 garlic clove, peeled and minced
- Salt to taste

- ❖ Place all ingredients into a deep salad bowl and toss gently. Taste for salt and season as needed.

Feel free to improve this salad by adding olives, fresh baby spinach leaves, fresh radishes, and other suitable vegan ingredients. You can also choose to omit some of the base recipe ingredients. It's all up to you.

27.   Salad of Roasted Banana Peppers with Garlic

This simple, delicious salad, captures the best of summer too.

- 7-10 whole red sweet banana peppers
- 4 garlic cloves, peeled and crushed
- 6 tbsp. vegetable oil
- 2 tbsp. vinegar
- Salt and pepper to taste

- ❖ Fire up your grill to high before putting the peppers on.
- ❖ Lay the peppers whole on the grill, making sure you do not overcrowd the grill.
- ❖ Cook until the skin is charred, about 20 minutes or longer, turning on each side to char the skin evenly.
- ❖ Make sure all skin is blackened before removing the peppers from the grill. If necessary, keep grilling longer.
- ❖ Remove from grill, and set on a rack to cool and drain.
- ❖ Peel the charred skins off, and wash. Drain again.
- ❖ In a salad bowl, make a marinade of oil, vinegar, garlic, and salt and pepper.
- ❖ Tip the peppers in and toss to cover evenly.

28.   Green Beans with Garlic Salad

This is a seasonal salad that takes advantage of that special time of the year when green beans are still tender, and therefore edible. It is a staple during Lent (cooked without oil), in the spring. Of course, you can use frozen green bean pods if you want to prepare this salad in the winter.

- 1 kg raw green bean pods – washed and ends trimmed
- 6 garlic cloves, minced finely
- 2 large tbsp. chopped parsley and dill

- 4 tbsp. sunflower oil (olive oil or canola oil can be used too)
- 2 tbsp. vinegar
- Salt and pepper to taste

- ❖ In a deep skillet, bring salted water to a boil.
- ❖ Make a marinade of oil, vinegar, garlic, parsley and dill. Season with salt and paper to taste.
- ❖ Tip in the bean pods. Cook until crisp-tender, but still bright green – for 6-7 minutes.
- ❖ Remove from heat, drain through a sieve, and place into a deep salad bowl.
- ❖ Pour the marinade over the beans while they are still hot. Toss gently to cover evenly. Taste for seasoning, and add more salt, pepper or vinegar if necessary.

Although it is not a traditional Romanian practice, you can replace the vinegar in this recipe with lemon juice. You can also sprinkle some chili flakes when you serve to add extra zing and color. Variations of this recipe may include a fresh tomato cut into small cubes and mixed in at the end. The dish is served at room temperature.

Another favorite during the Lent season (always cook without oil when you prepare a dish for Lent), this seasonal salad is a staple in Romanian kitchens from early spring until early autumn: as long as spring onions (alternatively, use chives) and dill grow naturally in the garden.

- 5-6 large potatoes, peeled and cubed
- 1 bunch fresh dill, chopped
- 4 spring onions, chopped

- 3 tbsp. sunflower oil
- Salt and pepper to taste
- Optional: 2 tbsp. vinegar

- ❖ In a large skillet, bring water and salt to a boil. Tip in the potatoes and cook over medium heat until you can pierce them with a fork – about 20 minutes.
- ❖ Remove the potatoes from heat, drain them through a sieve, and allow them to cool off.
- ❖ When the potatoes are cold, place them into a deep salad bowl. Add onions, dill, and oil. Season with salt and pepper to taste, and toss gently until all ingredients incorporate evenly.

Although it is not a traditional Romanian practice, you can also add 1 tbsp. of vinegar or lemon juice to the recipe to give the potatoes a fresh, sour zing. The dish is served cold.

30.   Homemade Sauerkraut

Another seasonal salad, typical in winter in Oltenia. It is made of traditional sauerkraut, which is finely cut cabbage fermented (pickled) in a special water and salt broth. It is available to purchase in good supermarkets, but don't buy the one prepared in vinegar. Instead, buy organic, salt-pickled sauerkraut or make your own.

How to Make Sauerkraut

Select a medium-sized cabbage head and chop it finely (julienne).

Place it into a deep bowl and add a large handful of finely chopped dill – this step is optional, for flavor. You can skip the dill.

Sprinkle 2 tablespoons of good natural sea salt over the cabbage, and, using your hands, massage it into the cabbage for about 10 minutes until the cabbage becomes watery, like coleslaw.

Place the cabbage into a mason jar, and tamp it down tightly with your fist. Pour any liquid released when you massaged it back over the cabbage. It is important that the cabbage is submerged in liquid while it is fermenting. If you don't have enough liquid, dissolve 1 teaspoon of salt in 1 cup of lukewarm water and add enough to cover the cabbage. Find a weight to keep the cabbage from floating while fermenting. (Romanians use clean branches of cherry tree bundled in a wreath and placed inside the jar to push down the cabbage.)

Cover the jar with a clean cloth and secure it with rubber band.

Over the next 24 hours, make sure the cabbage stays down. Press it down with the weight several times. This is when you start a process called "pitrocire." Pitrocire basically means that you immerse a drinking straw into the jar, deep into the cabbage and blow in the straw a few times, several times a day.

While the cabbage is fermenting keep the jar in a cool place, away from direct sunlight. The fermenting process takes at least 4 days, but you can continue the process for 10 days or longer, until the sauerkraut tastes good to you.

Note that bubbles or a white foam are a good sign during the fermentation process. You can remove the foam before refrigerating the sauerkraut. If the sauerkraut is molding, the process has failed.

When the sauerkraut achieves the desired taste, you can use it for a variety of dishes, including salads, ciorbe (soups), and main dishes. The liquid that results from fermenting the cabbage is often used in Romania to season ciorbe.

31.   Sauerkraut Salad

Raw sauerkraut is rich in glucosinolates and probiotic bacteria and has exceptional health benefits. The following recipe, a winter staple in Romanian homes, gives you all the health benefits you can possibly enjoy with a vegan diet.

- 300 g sauerkraut
- 1 tsp. sweet paprika powder
- 1 small bunch celery leaves, chopped finely
- 2 tbsp. sunflower oil
- Pepper to taste

❖ Place all ingredients in a deep salad bowl and mix well to blend all the flavors. Allow the salad to rest for at least 30 minutes before serving.

The salad is usually consumed between meals, but it can also be enjoyed as a palate cleanser at the beginning of a more consistent dinner. You can enhance it with tomato cubes or with 1 tbsp. of tomato paste. If you enjoy spicy foods, sprinkle your salad with chili flakes before serving.

VEGAN ROMANIA   MIHAELA LICA BUTLER

32.   Simple Mushroom Salad

Another favorite during the Lent season, this seasonal salad is a staple in Romanian kitchens from early spring until early autumn: as long as spring onions (alternatively use chives) and dill grow naturally in the garden.

- 12-16 table mushrooms, washed and stems removed
- 1 bunch fresh parsley, chopped

- 2 white onions, cut julienne
- 3 tbsp. sunflower oil
- 1 tbsp. vinegar
- Salt and pepper to taste

- ❖ In a large skillet, bring water, vinegar and salt to a boil. Tip in the mushrooms, and cook over medium heat for 15 minutes.
- ❖ Remove from heat, drain them through a sieve (don't discard the broth), and allow them to cool off.
- ❖ When they are cold, cut them into medium-thin slices, and put them into a deep salad bowl.
- ❖ In a small glass, prepare a sauce of 3 tbsp. oil (unless you prepare this for Lent, when you would skip the oil) and 3 tbsp. broth. Mix well.
- ❖ Pour the sauce over the mushrooms. Add onions and parsley and toss gently. Season with salt and pepper to taste. If necessary, sprinkle in more vinegar.

The dish is served cold as an appetizer, or as a side dish for main dishes such as stuffed eggplant, stuffed pepper, etc. You can also make it part of a mezze (appetizer).

33.   Traditional Zacuscă Salad

Romanians conserve the tastes of autumn and its finest flavors. The following is the recipe of a traditional Romanian bread spread called "zacuscă." The origins of the dish are Russian (закуска, zakuska) but the Romanian zacuscă recipe is significantly different from its Slavic relative.

- 3-4 kg fresh eggplants
- 1.5 kg fresh tomatoes
- 3 kg fresh red peppers
(called gogoșari or in the U.S., bell peppers. Alternatively, you could use other types of meaty peppers, like sweet red banana peppers)
- 1 kg onions
- 1 kg minced carrots
- 1 l sunflower oil (or virgin olive oil) taste
- Salt and pepper to taste

- ❖ Roast the eggplants and the peppers over an open flame (preferably a grill) until their skins blacken. Peel off the skins and wash the vegetable thoroughly with warm water.
- ❖ Mince the eggplants gently (don't use food processors. They transform the pulp into mush).
- ❖ Chop the pepper in small cubes and mix with the eggplant pulp.
- ❖ Peel off the tomatoes and mince them (alternatively, you could use 500 g of tomato paste, but the fresh paste adds a better taste).
- ❖ Mince onions and place them in a large pot. Add the minced carrots and the oil and allow them to cook until golden over medium heat.
- ❖ Add the mix of eggplant and pepper to the boiling oil and onion, tip in tomatoes, then season with salt and black pepper.
- ❖ Cook over low heat for about 2 hours, stirring repeatedly. Season again with salt and pepper to your taste. Refrigerate for 30 minutes before serving.

If you want to save this salad for the winter, spoon the mixture into sterilized jars, seal them and then boil the jars for about 20-30 minutes in a large water bath canner.

Allow the jars to cool in the same water.

Other recipes might include cooked beans, mushrooms, celery or other ingredients, and spices (according to taste).

It's really up to your imagination to improve this dish. You could add zucchini, for example, or even eliminate some of the ingredients mentioned above (like the carrots).

Some cooks replace eggplants with cooked beans, and so on. There's no unbreakable rule. Feel free to experiment until you find the right taste. The recipe above is my personal favorite.

Zacuscă can be served warm or cold, depending on your preference. It is a popular bread spread, usually in the winter. It can be served for breakfast, although this is not a general rule.

Soups and Ciorbe

A Romanian soup is a clear dish, with no added sour ingredients, while ciorbă (plural: ciorbe) is rich in vegetables and is enhanced with sour components, such as sauerkraut broth, lemon, green mirabelle plum paste, or barley bran borș. Many households use citric acid crystalline powder instead of any of the aforementioned ingredients. It's really up to you to decide what you prefer, and up to what's available where you live.

I prefer using a homemade mirabelle plum paste. This is the first recipe I will share with you, before any ciorbe.

Don't be surprised to find what you would usually define as a cream soup described as "ciorbă" in this book.

Also, this part of the traditional Romanian cuisine is where lovage (Levisticum officinale) comes in. It is widely used to boost the flavor of soups and ciorbe, even more so than parsley and dill.

You cannot expect many cream soups or cream ciorbe in Romanian cuisine. It is not in our tradition to puree vegetables. We like to see what we eat, plus... cooking without creaming saves time. There are a few exceptions, however.

Another important thing you need to know about our "ciorbe" is that they are a traditional daily meal in many Romanian homes. I respect this tradition. I still cook a different ciorbă, or soup, every day for my family. However, because I mainly create cream soups, based on my own whims, I only share traditional base recipes here for you to build upon.

Many of the recipes in this book (unless otherwise noted) are from Teleorman, as I remember them from my childhood when my grandmother, Victoria Ghețe, taught me how to cook.

34.   Mirabelle Paste for Ciorbă

You can always use other sour ingredients, like lemon and even vinegar, to add the final touch to a Romanian ciorbă, but nothing quite compares to a traditional mirabelle plum paste. This is fun and easy to make: you only need two ingredients…

- 1 kg mirabelle plums
- Water to boil

❖ Wash the mirabelles. Place them into a deep boiling pan, then cover up with water, about 2 cm, and bring to a boil over medium heat.

❖ Boil until very soft – the excess water needs to evaporate – then set aside to cool.

❖ Mash the mirabelles into a paste with a fork, carefully removing the pits. Bring to a boil again, just until hot.

❖ Place the paste into sterilized, dry jars, and sterilize for the winter. Ladle the hot mirabelle paste into hot sterilized jars, leaving 1/4-inch headspace.

❖ Wipe the rims thoroughly and screw on the lids.

❖ Place the jars in a deep boiling pot and cover completely with water.

❖ Cover the pot with a lid and bring to a boil over high heat, for 10 minutes or so.

❖ Turn off the heat and set aside for five to ten minutes.

❖ Remove the jars from the pot and allow them to rest undisturbed overnight.

35.   Onion and Cabbage Ciorbă

Hot, full of vitamins, and delicious. This is the perfect winter treat.

- 5 large onions, sliced into rings
- 1 leek, white part, sliced into rings
- 200 ml dry white wine (optional)
- ½ savoy cabbage, cut julienne
- 2 carrots, finely grated
- ½ cup fresh celery leaves, cut julienne
- ½ tsp black cumin seeds
- ½ tsp fennel seeds
- 2 tbsp. extra virgin olive oil
- Sauerkraut juice (to taste)
- 1½ liter water, boiling hot
- Salt and pepper to taste

- ❖ Preheat oil in a deep skillet, over medium heat.
- ❖ Add onions, leeks, cumin and fennel. Cook until translucent, stirring occasionally for about 7-8 minutes.
- ❖ Pour the white wine (or replace with 1 cup boiling water), reduce heat to minimum, and let simmer for a couple of minutes until the alcohol has evaporated.
- ❖ Add the cabbage, celery leaves and carrots, cover with hot water, add the sauerkraut broth, and let simmer for 7-9 minutes.
- ❖ Season with salt and pepper, and remove from heat.

Serve hot, garnished with chili flakes, with parsley leaves or with dill.

36.   Fresh Lettuce Ciorbă

This is a spring favorite, featuring garden fresh ingredients. You are unlikely to find this dish in many world cuisines. It is customary at the Easter table.

- 1 large head lettuce - chopped coarsely
- 1 bunch fresh radish leaves - chopped coarsely
- 1 bunch lovage - chop the stems, keep the leaves for last
- 1 bunch parsley - chop the stems, keep the leaves for last
- 1 large onion, finely chopped
- 3-4 garlic cloves, minced
- 1 fresh bell pepper, sliced thinly
- 2-3 spring onions, only the leaves, no whites, chopped
- 1 tablespoon olive oil
- Salt and pepper to taste
- 2 tbsp. Mirabelle paste or lemon juice
- 6 cups water (hot)

- ❖ In a deep soup pot sauté onion (without green onion) over medium heat, until golden (about 8 minutes, stirring frequently, to avoid browning).
- ❖ Add the garlic and the chopped stems of parsley and lovage. Continue sautéing for 2-3 more minutes.
- ❖ Pour the mixture over the fresh radish leaves and add a cup of water.
- ❖ Let simmer for 4-5 minutes.
- ❖ Add the rest of the water and bring to a boil.
- ❖ When the water boils add the rest of the ingredients (don't forget the mirabelle plum paste) and season to taste.
- ❖ Simmer for a couple of minutes, until the salad is wilted.

This tastes equally delicious hot or cold. Although we typically consume it around Easter, you can cook it any time when the ingredients are available. Some ingredients, such as radish leaves, can be left out. You will not achieve the authentic taste without lovage.

37.   Traditional Romanian Peas Ciorbă

Hot, full of vitamins, and delicious. This is the perfect winter treat. This recipe calls for dry peas, but you can also use frozen peas if you want the dish to get done faster. There will be a huge difference in taste, though.

- 1 large onion, finely chopped
- 2 garlic cloves, chopped
- 2 large carrots, sliced
- 1½ cup dry peas
- 1 can organic tomatoes
- 6 cups water

- 1 tablespoon canola oil
- 1 pinch Turmeric
- 1 teaspoon dry garden herbs mix
- Salt and pepper to taste

- ❖ Rinse the dry peas a couple of times and drain them well.
- ❖ Heat the oil in a deep skillet over medium heat.
- ❖ Add the onion, garlic and dry garden herbs. Cook for 6-8 minutes, stirring occasionally until the onions have softened.
- ❖ Add the carrots, the peas and the water. Bring to boil.
- ❖ Reduce the heat and simmer for about 1 hour 50 mins for dry peas. (Peas that were soaked overnight only need 1 hour to cook. Frozen peas only need 10-15 minutes.)
- ❖ Pour in the tomatoes. Season with turmeric.
- ❖ Continue to simmer for 10 more minutes before seasoning with salt and pepper to taste.
- ❖ If you like spicy food, add a pinch of cayenne pepper or hot paprika powder (hot pimento).
- ❖ Let set for 5 minutes before serving for the flavors to blend.

38.   Transylvania-Style Potato Ciorbă

We had to have this here… because it is simply delicious and because Transylvania is a REAL Romanian territory, not just a fantasy place imagined by Bram Stocker. No, this dish will not keep the vampires at bay (if you still choose to believe vampires exist), but it will warm you up in winter.

- 6 large potatoes, peeled and diced
- 2 onions, minced
- ½ tbsp. paprika powder
- 1 tbsp. fresh lovage, chopped or 1 tbsp. dried
- ½ tbsp. flour
- 1 tbsp. sunflower oil
- 4.5 l hot, boiling water
- Salt and pepper to taste

- ❖ Heat the oil in a deep skillet over medium heat and sauté onions until golden (or glassy). If you are using dry lovage instead of fresh, this is the time to put it in.
- ❖ Tip in the potatoes and continue cooking, stirring constantly, for about 10 minutes. Mix in the flour and paprika powder.
- ❖ Add boiling water and cover the pot with a lid. Let it cook slowly, stirring occasionally, until potatoes are boiled (about 20 minutes, until the potatoes can be easily pierced with a fork).
- ❖ Season with salt and pepper. Add fresh lovage (skip this if you used dried lovage). Remove from the heat and cover for 5 minutes, allowing the flavors to blend.

39.   Lentils and Garlic Ciorbă

This lentil ciorbă is nourishing, healthy and flavorful, the perfect winter treat, but equally delicious every season.

- 500 g lentils (green or brown)
- 1 large onion, peeled and minced
- 8 garlic cloves, peeled and minced

- 2 tbsp. olive oil
- 1 sprig of thyme
- 1 tsp. sweet paprika powder
- 2 l water
- Salt and pepper to taste.

- ❖ Bring the lentils to boil in water and a sprig of thyme.
- ❖ Allow the lentils to boil until soft, remove from heat, then remove the thyme sprig.
- ❖ In a deep skillet, preheat the oil with sweet paprika powder. Add minced onion and garlic. Cook until onions are soft, stirring frequently, for about 10 minutes.
- ❖ Pour the mixture over the lentil soup and continue to cook for 5 minutes, stirring frequently.
- ❖ Season with salt and pepper to taste.

This is a base recipe, which can be improved with added flavors such as chili flakes, fresh garden herbs, and so on. Serve hot, garnished with fresh lovage, or with fresh parsley.

40.   Red Lentils and Barley Ciorbă

This is a recipe cooked in Romanian monasteries. It is nourishing and filling, perfect for the colder seasons.

- 400 g red lentils
- 100 g barley
- 1 large onion, peeled and minced
- 2 garlic cloves, peeled and minced
- 4 tbsp. sunflower oil
- 200 ml tomato juice
- 1 tbsp. sweet paprika powder
- 1 tbsp. fresh oregano, minced
- 1 bunch fresh parsley, chopped
- 2 l water
- Salt and pepper to taste

- ❖ Preheat the oil in a deep skillet, over medium heat. Tip in the onions and sauté until translucent – for about 8 minutes, stirring occasionally.
- ❖ Add the garlic, oregano and paprika. Continue sautéing for two more minutes before you tip in the barley.
- ❖ Add water and bring to a boil. Barley takes longer than red lentils to cook, so give it about 40 minutes before you add the lentils and the tomato juice. Do not add any salt at this point.
- ❖ Continue boiling for 10 more minutes before you season your soup with salt and pepper. Remove from heat.
- ❖ Mix in the parsley. Allow the soup to rest for about 5 minutes before serving.

41.   Garden Oracle and Wild Garlic Ciorbă

This is probably one of those impossible Romanian recipes for those living in Western European countries, in the U.S., or elsewhere, where garden oracle is not known. Garden oracle, also called orach or mountain spinach, is basically an edible weed. But don't be fooled by its humble origins. This plant is versatile, tasty, and can be used raw (in salads) or cooked.

- 1 generous bunch fresh wild garlic leaves, washed and chopped
- 1 generous bunch fresh garden orache leaves, washed and chopped
- 1 zucchini, grated
- 2 large tomatoes, cut into small cubes

- 1 carrot, grated
- 1 onion, minced
- 3 tbsp. sunflower oil
- 2 tbsp. mirabelle plum paste
- 2 tbsp. white rice
- Salt and pepper to taste
- 1.5 l water – boiling hot

- Preheat the oil in a deep skillet over medium heat. Tip in the onions and the carrots. Sauté for about 8 minutes, stirring occasionally.
- Add water and allow to boil for 5 more minutes before you tip in the zucchini and tomatoes.
- Add the rice and boil for 10 minutes. Add the wild garlic and the fresh orache leaves. Boil for 5 to 7 more minutes.
- Season with mirabelle plum paste, salt and pepper.
- Remove from heat and set aside to rest for 5 minutes before serving.

There are variations to this soup. Some recipes do not call for zucchini; others use root parsley instead of carrot.

You can always improvise, adding in a few lettuce leaves, for example, or fresh spinach. Whatever you do, add the leafy greens last since they boil quickly. They lose their beautiful color and healthy nutrients if cooked longer than necessary.

42.   Beetroot and Vegetables Ciorbă

Romanians have their own equivalent to what Russians call "borscht," except that our beetroot ciorbă is very different. Traditionally it is served with sour cream. But vegans don't need to follow this tradition. This ciorbă stands on its own legs: it doesn't need animal fats to enhance its taste.

- 2 beetroots, peeled and cubed
- 2 potatoes, peeled and cubed
- 2 carrots, grated
- 2 onions, minced

- 2 tbsp. mirabelle plum paste, or lemon juice, or barley bran borş
- Salt and pepper to taste
- 1 bunch fresh parsley leaves, chopped
- 1.5 l water – boiling hot

❖ This is a one pot soup. Simply place all the vegetables into hot water and boil until tender (typically 35-40 minutes over medium heat would suffice).

❖ When the vegetables are soft, season with salt and pepper and add the sour ingredient of your choice. Remove from heat.

❖ Mix in the parsley. Allow the soup to rest for about 5 minutes before serving.

43.   Spinach Ciorbă

Spinach ciorbă is one of the staples of Romanian cuisine, due to its rich nutritional value. Get your lovage ready for this: the flavor given by this wonderful herb enhances the broth and makes your spinach ciorbă taste really authentic.

- 1 kg fresh baby spinach
- 2 carrots, grated
- 1 root parsley, grated
- 2 onions, peeled and minced
- 4 garlic cloves, peeled and minced
- 2 tbsp. rice
- 1 large tomato, cut into small cubes
- 2 tbsp. freshly chopped lovage leaves
- 2 tbsp. mirabelle plum paste (or lemon juice)
- 2 l water
- Salt to taste

- ❖ In a deep skillet filled half with water bring carrots, root parsley, onions and rice to a boil. Cook for 20 minutes, until the vegetables are tender.
- ❖ Tip in the baby spinach. Cook for 10 more minutes.
- ❖ Add tomato and garlic. Continue cooking for about 5 more minutes.
- ❖ Remove from heat. Add mirabelle paste, lovage leaves. Season with salt to taste.
- ❖ Allow the soup to rest in the pot for five minutes before serving. This helps the flavors blend.

44.   Zucchini and Potato Ciorbă

This is pure comfort food: it is a light ciorbă, perfect for the Lent season, but also popular in warm summer months, autumn and winter. Call it the "all-season-fit."

- 3 zucchini, cubed
- 2 large potatoes, cubed
- 1 root parsley, grated
- 1 onion, peeled and minced
- 2 garlic cloves, peeled and minced
- 2 large tomatoes, cut into small cubes
- 2 tbsp. freshly chopped parsley
- 1 tbsp. mirabelle paste
- 2 l water
- Salt and pepper to taste

- ❖ Bring zucchini, potatoes, onion, and root parsley to boil over medium heat. Cook until the vegetables are tender, for about 20 minutes.
- ❖ Tip in the garlic. Add the tomatoes. Season with lemon, salt and pepper to taste. Cook for 10 more minutes.
- ❖ Remove from heat. Add parsley and allow the soup to rest in the pot for five minutes before serving.

45. Tomato Ciorbă

Tomato soups are traditional in many countries, but the Romanian variant has some particularities. It is a summer, autumn, and winter favorite, excellent when you feel a bit under the weather. I remember my grandma cooking this for me to recover after the flu.

- 8 large tomatoes, quartered
- 1 carrot, grated
- 1 root parsley, grated
- 1 tbsp. flour
- 100 g rice

- 2 tbsp. sunflower oil
- 1 red bell pepper
- 2 l hot water
- 1 tbsp. unrefined sugar
- Salt to taste

- ❖ Sprinkle the tomatoes with salt. Set them aside for 30 minutes.
- ❖ After 30 minutes, heat the oil in a deep skillet over medium-low heat. Add the flour to make a roux-style paste.
- ❖ Add the carrot and root parsley. Continue cooking for about 10 minutes, stirring frequently, before adding the water. It is important that your flour does not burn. If it starts browning, ladle in a bit of water and stir.
- ❖ Pour in the rest of the hot water. Add tomatoes and red bell pepper. Let cook for 30 minutes.
- ❖ In the meantime, boil the rice separately. Add 3 measures of water for a measure of rice. Don't worry if the rice is too runny – you will have to wash it thoroughly in cold water when it's done. This recipe does not call for sticky rice.
- ❖ When the vegetables are tender, puree them through a sieve, broth and all, just to make sure your soup doesn't contain any tomato seeds or skins.
- ❖ Bring to a boil again, then add sugar and salt to taste. Cook for 5 minutes before you add the rice.
- ❖ Remove from heat. Allow to rest in the pot for five minutes before serving.

Serve hot, garnished with fresh parsley or dill.

46.   White Beans Ciorbă

This is a traditional dish from Moldova county, where it is called borş. Variations of this classic exist all over Romania.

- 300 g white dry beans
- 1 carrot, grated
- 1 root parsley, grated
- 1 parsnip, grated
- 2 onions, peeled and minced
- 5 garlic cloves, peeled and minced

- 1 sprig of thyme
- 1 bunch fresh lovage
- 800 ml borş
- 4 tbsp. sunflower oil
- 2 l water
- Salt to taste

- ❖ Soak the beans in water for about 6 hours before cooking them. Soaking them too long (as in overnight) may cause them to ferment, which destroys their flavor.
- ❖ In a large pot place one part beans and three parts water. Add the bay leaves, then bring gently to boil. Cook for about 40 minutes before you add the rest of the vegetables. Romanians typically use Phaseolus vulgaris beans (the common beans), which need about 1 hour to soften.
- ❖ Add the borş. If you don't have borş, use sauerkraut broth instead, but only 400 ml.
- ❖ Season the soup with salt. Add the oil. Allow it to simmer for 10 more minutes.
- ❖ Remove from heat and serve hot, sprinkled with fresh lovage.

47.   Stinging Nettles Ciorbă

This is a simple, basic recipe, with many different variations across the country. But, my base recipe, which comes from Teleorman, is, naturally, my favorite, especially since it doesn't call for sour cream or other taste enhancers based on animal fats.

Stinging nettles are available at the farmers' markets in Romania, but some people, including myself, prefer to pick them themselves, in the forest. Don't attempt to pick up nettles with your bare hands if you are not used to the sting. Some people may have violent reactions to it, with large, painful bumps. I know just how to grab the plant to avoid the sting. Use thick household rubber gloves when handling these pesky leaves. They are safe when boiled and have a taste similar to spinach.

- ½ kg stinging nettles
- 1 onion, peeled and minced
- 3 tbsp. sunflower oil (or canola or olive oil)
- 2 tbsp. rice
- 2 l water
- 1 tbsp. mirabelle paste
- 1 bunch fresh lovage
- 1 tbsp. flour
- 1 tsp. sweet paprika powder
- Salt and pepper to taste

- ❖ Wash the nettles well in plenty of water. Nettles are home to a variety of butterfly larvae, which will be killed by boiling, but it's better to wash them carefully before use.
- ❖ In a deep skillet, bring water and salt to a boil before you toss in the nettles. Cook over medium heat, covered, until the nettles are soft and tender – about 30 minutes.
- ❖ Add the rice and continue cooking.
- ❖ In the meantime, in a separate skillet, heat the oil and sauté the onion with the sweet paprika for about 10 minutes, stirring frequently until the onion becomes translucent.
- ❖ Tip in the flour and stir to make a roux-style paste.
- ❖ Ladle some stinging nettles broth over the roux and stir well to obtain a sauce with the consistency of a gravy.
- ❖ Pour the gravy over the boiling stinging nettles, add the mirabelle plum paste, and season with salt and pepper to taste.
- ❖ Tip in the lovage before serving.

48.   Patience Dock Ciorbă

This is another dish specific to Oltenia. It is perfect for the spring. I am forced to plant patience dock (Rumex patientia) in my garden, as it is not available in store where I live. The recipe also calls for garden sorrel (Rumex acetosa), which I introduced in a previous recipe. On the chance that you like gardening as much as I do and you want to try something unlike anything else, here's my grandma's own recipe.

- 200 g patience dock
- 100 g sorrel
- 1 onion (or 4 spring onions), peeled and minced
- 2 garlic cloves, peeled and minced
- ½ bunch fresh lovage
- ½ bunch fresh parsley
- 2 tbsp. mirabelle plum paste
- 4 tbsp. sunflower oil
- 2 tbsp. rice
- 1.5 l water (hot)
- Salt to taste

- ❖ Wash patience dock and sorrel well, trim and chop them coarsely.
- ❖ In a deep skillet preheat oil and sauté onion until translucent, stirring to avoid burning for about 8 minutes.
- ❖ Tip in the garlic and cook for 2 more minutes.
- ❖ Add the patience dock and sorrel. Stir for a couple of minutes, until the greens are wilted.
- ❖ Add water and rice. Cook for 20 minutes before adding parsley and lovage. Cook for another 2 minutes.
- ❖ Season with mirabelle plum paste, salt and pepper to taste. Remove from heat.

Serve hot.

49.   Traditional Vegetable Ciorbă

This has so many variations around the country, that it is very hard to pinpoint it on the map. It is pretty much a minestrone, but pasta and rice are optional in Romanian cuisine. Many other things are optional as well. Some regions add a beaten egg at the end while the broth is still boiling, which makes the ciorbă richer, thicker (and obviously non-vegan). For the purpose of serving a vegan dish, we'll stick to the base recipe, as I remember it from my childhood.

- 1 kohlrabi turnip, peeled and cubed
- 2 bell peppers, deseeded and cubed
- 1 zucchini, cubed
- 2 large potatoes, peeled and cubed
- 1 carrot, cubed
- 1 root parsley, cubed
- 1 handful lovage leaves, chopped
- 1 handful parsley leaves, chopped
- ½ celeriac, peeled and cubed
- 2 large tomatoes, peeled and cubed
- 3 tbsp. oil
- 1 onion, peeled and cut julienne
- 2 tbsp. mirabelle plum paste (or lemon juice, or 1 ladle sauerkraut broth)
- 2 liter water, boiling hot
- Salt and pepper to taste

- ❖ Preheat oil in a deep skillet, over medium heat.
- ❖ Add onions, carrot, root parsley, bell peppers and celeriac. Cook, stirring often, until the onion is translucent, about 10 minutes.
- ❖ Add hot water, kohlrabi, zucchini and potatoes. Cook until the veggies are soft for about 25 minutes.
- ❖ Add the tomatoes and continue boiling for 5 more minutes before you tip in the mirabelle plum paste.
- ❖ Season with salt and pepper. Add lovage and parsley. Remove from heat.

If you like spicy foods, you can always enhance your ciorbă with spicy paprika powder. If so, add the paprika at the beginning, together with the onion, carrot, root parsley, celeriac and bell peppers. Serve hot.

50.   Easy Mushroom Ciorbă

Ordinary champignon mushrooms are so versatile. I like them raw, steamed, sautéed, grilled, and even boiled. This recipe is customary in the Lent season or spring. It takes no time to cook. It is light and full of flavor.

- 500 white champignon mushrooms, washed, stems removed, and sliced
- 2 carrots, grated
- 1 onion, peeled and minced
- 5 garlic cloves, peeled and minced
- 1 root parsley, grated
- 1 bunch parsley, leaves chopped
- 4 tbsp. sunflower oil (or your favorite cooking oil)
- 2 liters water, cold
- Salt and pepper to taste

- ❖ Preheat oil in a deep skillet, over medium heat. Add salt, onion, carrot and root parsley. Sauté until all vegetables are soft, for about 10 minutes. (Sauté in water if you make this for Lent or fasting.)
- ❖ Tip in sliced mushrooms and garlic. Add water. Season with salt and pepper and bring to a boil.
- ❖ Simmer for 15 minutes over medium heat before you add parsley leaves. Remove from heat.

51.   Zucchini and Eggplant Ciorbă

This is a traditional monastery recipe from Vrancea County. It is a refreshing recipe, healthy and full of flavor.

- 2 zucchinis, peeled and cubed
- 2 eggplants, rubbed with salt, then cubed
- 4 carrots, grated
- 1 parsley root, grated
- ½ celeriac, grated
- 3 onions, peeled and minced
- 1 potato, peeled and cubed

- 1 bell pepper, trimmed, deseeded and cubed
- 1 root parsley, grated
- 1 bunch parsley, leaves chopped
- 4 tbsp. sunflower oil
- 2 tbsp. mirabelle plum paste
- 2 liter water, cold
- Salt and pepper to taste

- ❖ Preheat oil in a deep skillet, over medium heat. Add salt, onion, bell pepper, celeriac, carrot and root parsley. Sauté until all vegetables are soft, for about 10 minutes.
- ❖ Tip in cubed potato, add water, and bring to a boil. Simmer for 15 minutes over medium heat.
- ❖ Add zucchini and eggplant. Continue simmering for 10 more minutes before you add mirabelle plum paste.
- ❖ Taste the broth for salt and pepper. Season as needed.
- ❖ Remove from heat. Tip in the parsley and cover, allowing the ciorbă to rest for 2-3 minutes before serving it.

52. Simple Potato Ciorbă

A traditional monastery recipe from the historic region of Moldovia, this recipe is a staple for many Romanian households. There are countless variations of this dish, but even if you keep it simple it will still taste delicious.

- 6 large potatoes, peeled and cubed
- 1 carrot, grated
- ½ celeriac, peeled and grated
- 2 onions, peeled and minced

- 2 tbsp. sunflower oil (or canola oil)
- 2 l water
- Salt to taste

- ❖ Preheat oil in a deep skillet, over medium heat. Add onion, celeriac and carrot. Sauté until all vegetables are soft, for about 10 minutes.
- ❖ Tip in cubed potato, add water, and bring to a boil. Simmer for 25 minutes over medium heat.
- ❖ Taste the broth for salt. Season as needed.
- ❖ Remove from heat, tip in the parsley, and serve hot.

53.   White Cabbage Ciorbă

A healthy dish, rich in vitamins, the white cabbage ciorbă is believed to assist in weight loss diets. It is often made with meat-based broths. Traditionally, this can be a fasting dish when you cook it without oil.

- 1 cabbage, cut julienne
- 1-2 red onions, peeled and cut julienne
- 2 tbsp. oil
- 2 carrots, grated
- 1 root parsley, peeled and grated
- ½ celeriac, peeled and grated
- 1 bell pepper, trimmed, deseeded and cut julienne
- 3-4 large tomatoes, cubed

- 1 tbsp. thyme
- 3 l water
- 1 bay leaf
- 1 tbsp. sweet paprika powder
- 1 tsp. citric acid crystals (optional)
- Salt and pepper to taste
- Fresh parsley leaves to garnish

- ❖ Preheat oil in a deep skillet (with a capacity of at least 5 l) over medium heat. Add onion, celeriac, parsley, bell pepper and carrot. Sauté until all vegetables are soft, for about 10 minutes.
- ❖ Ladle in some water. Allow the vegetables to simmer for about 10 more minutes.
- ❖ Add tomatoes and cabbage, plus bay leaf, thyme and sweet paprika. Pour the rest of the water over the mixture.
- ❖ Reduce heat to medium. Cover the pot with a lid. Simmer for 30 minutes, stirring occasionally until the cabbage is soft.
- ❖ Season with salt and pepper. You can also add one teaspoon citric acid crystals to give your dish that extra zing.
- ❖ Garnish with fresh parsley leaves and serve hot.

54.   Sauerkraut Ciorbă

A winter favorite, the traditional sauerkraut ciorbă is made with smoked meats. But during Lent a vegan, oil-free version exists and it is equally delicious. See how to make sauerkraut in the previous chapter, Appetizers and Salads, if you cannot find it in store where you live.

- 500 g sauerkraut
- 1 onion, peeled and cut julienne
- 3 garlic cloves, peeled and minced
- 2 tbsp. oil
- 2 carrots, grated
- 1 root parsley, peeled and grated

- 1 tbsp. dry dill
- 2 tbsp. tomato paste
- 2 l water
- 1 bay leaf
- 1 tbsp. sweet paprika powder
- Pepper to taste

- ❖ Preheat oil in a deep skillet over medium heat. Add root parsley and carrot. Sauté for about 10 minutes.
- ❖ Tip in the onion and garlic with 2 tablespoons of tomato paste. Sprinkle the dill and the sweet paprika over them. Reduce the heat to medium. Continue cooking, stirring frequently, for the next 10 minutes.
- ❖ Add sauerkraut, water, and the bay leaf. Cover the skillet with a lid. Simmer for 30 minutes, stirring occasionally.
- ❖ Season with pepper.
- ❖ Garnish with fresh dill, if available, and serve hot.

55.   Stuffed Peppers Ciorbă

Stuffed peppers are a traditional Romanian specialty, which can be cooked either with a broth, as with ciorbă, or with a rich tomato sauce as a main dish. Traditionally, peppers are stuffed with meat and rice, however, Lent variations exist and are ideal for a vegan diet, too.

For the stuffed peppers:

- 6-8 bell peppers
- 2 leeks, washed, trimmed and minced
- 4-5 carrots, grated
- 100 g rice
- 2 tbsp. yellow maize flour
- 500 g mushrooms, minced
- 1 tbsp. fresh dill
- 1 tbsp. fresh parsley
- Salt and pepper to taste

For the ciorbă:

- 3-4 large tomatoes, sliced
- 2 red onions, peeled and minced
- 1 carrot, grated
- 200 ml tomato juice
- 2 l water warm
- Salt and pepper to taste
- 1 tsp. citric acid crystals (or 2 tbsp. mirabelle plum paste)

- ❖ Preheat oil in a deep skillet over medium heat. Sauté the leeks for about 10 minutes.
- ❖ Add grated carrots, mushrooms and rice. Allow to cook, stirring frequently, until the mushrooms release their water and the rice is half done.
- ❖ Remove from heat and allow the mixture to cool off.
- ❖ In the meantime, prepare your bell peppers. Cut a thin slice from the stem end of each bell pepper to remove the top. Carefully remove the seeds and the membranes. Rinse well. Return to the mixture of mushrooms and rice, add dill, parsley, maize flour, salt and pepper. Mix well.
- ❖ Stuff the peppers with the mixture, but leave a small space at the top since the rice will continue to expand.
- ❖ Layer a deep, non-stick soup pot with tomato slices. Carefully place the stuffed peppers on top, making sure that they remain vertical.
- ❖ Mix water, mirabelle paste (or citric acid) and tomato juice. Pour the mixture over the peppers, carefully, to fully cover them.
- ❖ Add grated carrot. Season with salt and pepper to taste. Cover the pot with a lid. Simmer at medium-low heat for about an hour. Garnish with fresh parsley and serve hot.

This dish is traditional in mid-summer and early autumn. It is an easy dish, ready in minutes. It is very refreshing. As usual, the base recipe can be enhanced with additional ingredients. Non-vegans can serve it with cream.

- 500 g wax beans, washed and trimmed
- 1 onion, peeled and minced
- 3 garlic cloves, peeled and minced
- 2 tbsp. oil
- 1 carrot, grated
- 1 large potato, peeled and cubed

- 2 l water
- 1 bay leaf
- 1 tbsp. fresh lemon juice
- 1 bunch fresh dill
- Salt to taste

- ❖ Preheat oil in a deep skillet over medium heat. Add carrot, onion and garlic. Sauté for about 10 minutes.
- ❖ Tip in the potato and wax beans, and the water. Continue cooking for about 20 minutes, until the vegetables are nice and tender.
- ❖ Season with salt to taste. Add lemon juice and remove from heat.
- ❖ Garnish with fresh dill and serve hot.

Variations of this recipe call for 1 large tomato, peeled and cubed. The tomato is usually added about five minutes before the dish is seasoned and removed from the heat. Occasionally, you can replace the dill with parsley or finely chopped lovage.

Mămăliga – the bread of gold – (also known as polenta) is a traditional Romanian staple. It is considered an alternative to bread in poor rural areas. It is cooked in many homes and it is made of yellow maize flour. It is pretty similar to grits. There are many uses for this humble dish. You will even find it in first class restaurants, usually described as polenta, since the word "mămăligă" has some negative implications. Romanians have been labeled as mămăligari (eaters of polenta) for generations because the dish is so common in the country. Because the usual mămăligă is soft, a mămăligar would also be "soft," cowardly, and easy to push around. Of course, this label is a great injustice to the spirit and the true character of the Romanian people. There's also that old saying that someone is "so poor that he doesn't even have mămăligă to eat."

Mămăliga is not, as some describe it, "Romania's answer to polenta." It is a national dish, with a history that spans over 400 years. And it was the Jewish Romanian immigrants who brought mămăliga with them to the U.S. in the late 19th century.*

Varieties of mămăligă are found in many other countries, including Moldova, Bulgaria, Hungary, Italy, Germany, Switzerland, Austria, Croatia, Slovenia, Serbia and Ukraine, as well as Latin countries such as Mexico, Brazil, Uruguay, Argentina and Venezuela. This only means that basic cereal porridges are one thing that is common to many cultures of the world.

The recipe for mămăligă is the same all over the country: yellow maize flour, water and salt. There are, however, two styles of mămăligă, based on the cooking time. One is hard and can be cut. The other has the consistency of a thick porridge.

This very short chapter explores both variants of the dish, and includes serving ideas. There is also a third, surprise recipe based on mămăligă.

---

* *Gil Marks, Encyclopedia of Jewish Food, Houghton Mifflin Harcourt; 1 edition (August 25, 2010)*

57.   Romanian Mămăligă (Bread-Style)

Whatever quantity mămăligă you want to make, remember this very simple rule: to every measure of maize flour, add four measures of water. For example, for one cup flour, add four cups water, and so on. The following recipe is intended to feed a family of six people. Whatever you decide, keep in mind that, although a very simple dish, mămăliga requires some skill and a wooden spoon with a very long handle.

- 400 g yellow maize flour
- 1600 ml water
- Salt to taste

- ❖ Bring salted water to a boil in a skillet deep enough to hold all the ingredients, leaving room to add more if necessary.
- ❖ Reduce the heat to low. Add the maize flour slowly, stirring constantly, so that the flour doesn't form lumps. Be careful when you stir. The hot vapors of the mixture can cause serious burns. Also, as the mixture thickens, you will notice that it continues to release hot vapors and mash forming bubbles, which pop pretty much like a volcano. Stir constantly to prevent the said volcano from becoming big enough to mess up your entire stove in the process.
- ❖ It takes about 40 minutes of cooking for the mămăligă to be ready. Remove from heat and overturn the skillet on a wooden surface. Be careful, as the hot mămăligă can burn your skin.
- ❖ The mămăligă should keep the approximate shape of the skillet and remain firm on the plate. Wait for 10 minutes for the mămăligă to cool off before you cut it with a string (mămăligă sticks to metal surfaces, therefore a knife is not recommended).

Mămăligă is fat-free, cholesterol-free, and high in -fiber. Therefore it is often recommended instead of bread or rice. It replaces bread, so it is not a side dish. You can consume it with a variety of main dishes, including the famous Romanian sarmale (stuffed cabbage). It can also be enjoyed with a special dip, called "mujdei de ustoroi," which is healthy, vegan, and yes... garlicky. If you want a recipe that requires less cooking time the result will be a porridge-style mămăligă, equally healthy and delicious.

58.   Hurried Romanian Mămăligă (Porridge-Style)

The base mămăligă recipe always requires four measures of water for every measure of yellow maize flour.

- 400 g yellow maize flour
- 1600 ml water
- Salt to taste

❖   Repeat all the steps mentioned in the previous mămăligă recipe, but cook the flour for only 25 minutes. You will obtain a porridge-style mămăligă, which cannot be overturned on a wooden surface. Just spoon it onto plates and serve.

This softer, porridge-style mamăliga has the same nutritional values as the harder version. It can be used to replace bread and served with a variety of sauces and main dishes. Non-vegans usually enjoy it with cheese and eggs, but there are many ways for vegans to enjoy it too: with spinach, nettles, sarmale (stuffed cabbage), and other traditional dishes.

59.   Grilled Romanian Mămăligă (polenta)

You need cold slices of bread-style mămăligă for this dish. Refer to recipe No. 57 to learn how to make hard mămăligă. You can always use day-old mămăligă for this recipe.

- 8-10 hard mămăligă slices
- 2 tbsp. sunflower oil
- Salt and pepper to taste

❖   Preheat your grill. Brush each slice of mămăligă with oil on both sides. Season with salt and pepper to taste.

❖   Grill each mămăligă slice about 3 minutes on both sides. Don't overdo it. The mămăligă is already cooked. You can grill the slices longer, but make sure the maize does not burn.

This is an original, fun way to use cold mămăliga leftovers. The grilled mămăligă can be served, instead of bread, with the usual suspects: sauerkraut, sarmale (stuffed cabbage), beans, spinach, and so on.

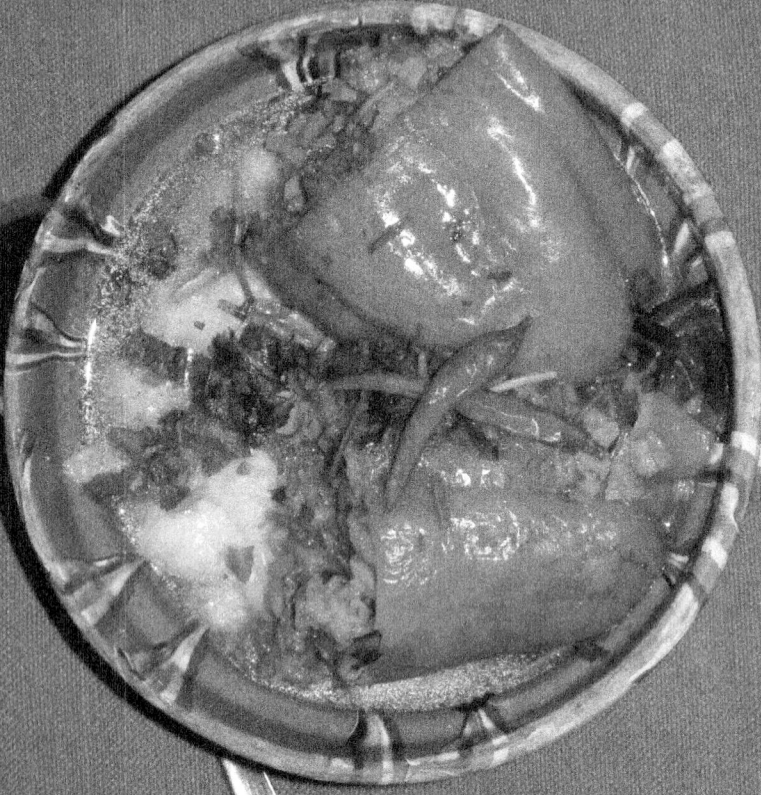

Vegan Main Dishes

Oceanographer Jacques Yves Cousteau once said, "I would say that not only does the world in fact know nothing about Romania, but neither do you, Romanians, recognize miracles. When it comes to cuisine, at least, you are very, very rich in your so-called poverty." And he was so right.

To his words, I would add that Romanians themselves know very little about the rich plant-based cuisine of their own country, preferring instead foods that are rich in animal fats. For many, Lent is an occasion for complaining about "what should I cook today." When it comes to cookbooks focused exclusively on traditional Romanian vegan recipes, the market lacks what's needed. Cookbooks today borrow a lot from the cuisines of the world, introducing dishes that were virtually unknown 20 or 30 years ago in my country. You also have to consider that many Romanians also fast during the week on Wednesdays and Fridays, and in the Advent season before Christmas. A Romanian Orthodox may fast up to 192 days out of the entire year, usually counting on the same simple foods, without caring too much about diversifying his or her diet. No long fasting periods happen during the summer, when the abundance of fresh produce allows creativity in the kitchen.

It takes a great effort to find recipes that are truly authentic and as good as grandma's. You can always count on food served in monasteries to be as close to the traditional regional recipes as possible. Nevertheless, there's still plenty to choose from to make a healthy vegan main dish. Some of the following recipes are adapted from a non-vegan recipe to suit a vegan diet. Also, please note: eating vegan is not fasting if you use oil to cook. If you want to use any of the following recipes for fasting, simply cook them, when possible, without oil.

Last, but not least, many of the Romanian foods known today were influenced by the cuisines of Greece, Turkey, Bulgaria, Russia, Hungary, and so on. Don't be surprised to notice similarities.

60.   Rice and Spinach

Traditional in some Muntenian monasteries, this recipe is perfect for a vegan diet. You can always use risotto rice to prepare it, but Romanians use short-grain rice, which becomes really sticky when cooked.

- 1 kg fresh spinach, washed and trimmed
- 200 g rice
- 2 onions, peeled and minced
- 6-8 garlic cloves, peeled and minced

- 2 tbsp. sunflower oil
- 400 ml water
- Salt to taste

- ❖ Preheat the oven at 200°C/400°F.
- ❖ In a deep oven-safe skillet, sauté onion and garlic in oil over medium heat, stirring occasionally, until they become golden.
- ❖ Add the spinach, rice and water. Cook for about 10 minutes before seasoning with salt and placing the skillet in the oven. Alternatively, you can ladle the mixture in ceramic ramekins.
- ❖ Bake for 15-20 minutes, until the rice is tender. Serve hot.

To cook this recipe without oil, simply boil the rice and spinach for 8 minutes, then add the onion and garlic before you place the dish into the oven. Mix the ingredients well to incorporate the minced onion and garlic. This is a main dish, standalone recipe, but it can be accompanied by a fresh salad. It can also follow a hearty ciorbă.

61.   Spinach with Tomatoes and Garlic

Spinach is such a healthy, versatile vegetable, but not all people enjoy its metallic taste. This recipe changes things. Surprisingly enough it is enjoyed by many children in Romania.

- 2 kg fresh spinach, washed and trimmed
- 4-5 large tomatoes, peeled and cubed
- 2 onions, peeled and minced
- 6 garlic cloves, peeled and minced
- 2 tbsp. sunflower oil
- Water to boil the spinach
- Ice cold water to immerse the spinach after boiling
- Salt to taste

- ❖ Bring water to a boil in a deep skillet over medium heat.
- ❖ Add in the spinach. Allow to cook for about 2 minutes, until the leaves are wilted.
- ❖ Drain through a sieve, then immerse in ice cold water. This prevents the spinach from changing its bright, beautiful green color into a disgusting, mushy khaki. Allow the spinach about 5 minutes in this water before draining it well for the second time.
- ❖ Chop the spinach and set aside.
- ❖ Sauté onion in oil over medium heat in a separate skillet, for about 10 minutes, until the onion becomes golden and soft.
- ❖ Tip in the tomatoes. Continue cooking for about 5 minutes before adding the chopped spinach, salt and garlic.
- ❖ Cook for 5-7 more minutes, then remove from heat.

This is a standalone recipe, delicious with mămăligă (polenta). Of course, it can also be served with bread. You can even enjoy it cold in the morning, on bread, as a spread. Variations of this recipe eliminate the tomatoes and use a roux-type of base, made of oil, onion, and flour with one cup of water, or one cup of vegetable stock. The chopped spinach is added to this sauce, together with the garlic, to form a creamy main dish. It is served on porridge-style mămăligă.

62.   Spinach with Mushrooms and Garlic

This is pretty much a variation of the previous recipe and a personal favorite. It can be done with any kind of mushrooms, but I prefer a mix of wild mushrooms from the can (as cans are strictly controlled by experts and are safer than buying mushrooms fresh from the farmers' markets).

- 2 kg fresh spinach, washed and trimmed
- 6 garlic cloves, peeled and minced
- 600 g canned mushrooms, drained
- 4 tbsp. sunflower oil
- 2 tbsp. flour
- 3 tbsp. tomato juice, or 1 tbsp. tomato paste

- 1 bunch mixed herbs: lovage, dill and parsley, chopped
- Water to boil the spinach
- Ice cold water to immerse the spinach after boiling
- 200 ml boiling hot water
- Salt to taste

- ❖ Bring water to a boil in a deep skillet over medium heat.
- ❖ Add in the spinach. Allow to cook for about 2 minutes, until the leaves are wilted.
- ❖ Drain through a sieve, then immerse in ice cold water. This prevents the spinach from changing its bright, beautiful green color into a disgusting, mushy khaki. Allow the spinach about 5 minutes in this water before draining it well for the second time.
- ❖ Chop the spinach and set aside.
- ❖ Sauté garlic in oil over medium heat in a separate skillet for about 2 minutes, then add the flour, stirring constantly, to form the base for a roux.
- ❖ Add the tomato juice and the mushrooms and 200 ml of boiling hot water. Cook for 10 minutes before adding the chopped spinach.
- ❖ Cook for 5-7 more minutes, then season with salt to taste. Tip in the herbs. Mix well and remove from heat.

Served with any type of mămăligă or bread. This is a delicious main dish, rich in iron and protein.

63.   Nettles with Garlic

A personal favorite, this recipe is traditional in the spring when the nettles just start growing. You would normally pick just the tender tips of the nettles, wearing thick gardening gloves. But young leaves are also fine if the patch you harvest doesn't have enough of the tender tops.

- 1 kg fresh nettles, washed several times
- 6 garlic cloves, peeled and minced
- 1 onion, peeled and minced
- 4 tbsp. sunflower oil
- 1 tbsp. flour
- Water to boil the nettles
- Salt to taste

- ❖ Bring salted water to a boil in a deep skillet over medium heat.
- ❖ Add in the nettles and allow to cook for about 10 minutes, until the leaves are tender.
- ❖ Drain through a sieve, but do not discard the broth.
- ❖ Chop the nettles and set aside.
- ❖ Sauté onion in oil over medium heat in a separate skillet for about 10 minutes, then add the flour, stirring constantly, to form the base for a roux.
- ❖ Ladle in some nettle broth and stir well to form the roux-sauce.
- ❖ Add garlic and nettles and stir well. If the paste obtained is too thick, ladle in more nettle broth.
- ❖ Cook for 15 more minutes, adding more broth as needed, then season with salt to taste. The consistency of the dish should be similar to a not-so-thick pesto.

Served with any type of mămăligă, this is a delicious standalone main dish. Non-vegans enjoy this with fried eggs, or as a side dish for meat-based dishes, especially lamb. You can also mix some of this nettle base with spaghetti for a delicious, healthy, pasta-special.

In many parts of Romania, the remaining nettle broth is consumed hot with some salt, instead of tea. It is believed that nettle broth is very healthy.

64.   Young Zucchini with Dill

Young zucchini (or baby zucchini) are typically small plants that still have leftovers of the flowering part attached to the outer end. This is a wonderfully refreshing dish in late spring, usually cooked with cream, but adapted for a vegan diet in this book.

- 20 baby zucchini, ends trimmed and washed
- 2 garlic cloves, peeled and minced
- 4 tbsp. sunflower oil

- 1 tbsp. flour
- 1 bunch fresh dill
- Salt to taste

- ❖ Preheat oven at 200° C, 400° F.
- ❖ First pat the baby zucchini dry with kitchen towels.
- ❖ Preheat oil over medium heat in a deep, large skillet. Place the zucchini in carefully to fit them in. Typically, all zucchini should fit. If they don't, leave some aside for a different recipe.
- ❖ Fry zucchini on all sides until they become golden, then ladle in some hot water. Cover with a lid. Reduce heat to low.
- ❖ Cook zucchini until done (they should pierce easily with a fork all the way through).
- ❖ Drain through a sieve, but do not discard the broth.
- ❖ Don't wash the skillet. Instead, sauté garlic with oil for two minutes before adding flour and stirring to get the base for a roux. Ladle in the broth of the zucchini and stir for 5 minutes to get a thick sauce. Season with salt to taste.
- ❖ Place the zucchini in an oven-friendly ramekin.
- ❖ Pour the sauce over the zucchini.
- ❖ Put the ramekin in the oven and bake for 10-15 minutes.
- ❖ Sprinkle with fresh dill before serving hot.

This is a nice, light, and filling dish. Use a side made of lentils or serve with a fresh salad.

65.   Zucchini Pilaf

Pilaf is a recipe of Greek origin. It is usually made with meat (chicken), but it can also be adapted for a vegan diet. It is pretty similar to the famous Italian risotto.

- 2 large zucchinis with the ends trimmed, sliced thinly
- 2 large onions, peeled and minced
- 150 g long grain rice
- 4 tbsp. sunflower oil
- 400 ml vegetable stock
- 1 bunch fresh parsley, chopped
- Juice from ½ lemon (optional)
- Salt to taste

- ❖ In a deep skillet, preheat oil. Tip in the onion and sauté for 10 minutes over medium heat until onion is soft and golden.
- ❖ Add sliced zucchini and rice. Cover with vegetable stock. Season with salt to taste. Cook for 15 to 20 minutes, stirring occasionally until the rice absorbs the liquid and the zucchini is tender and easily pierced with a fork.
- ❖ Remove from heat. Add the parsley. Fluff the rice with a fork. Adding lemon juice at this point is optional (not traditional in our cuisine, but it gives the dish a special zing).

A great standalone main dish, you can also enjoy this as a side to main dishes like stuffed eggplant or stuffed peppers, for example. As a standalone dish, zucchini pilaf is usually served with a fresh lettuce salad.

66.   Zucchini and Tomato Stew

This is an easy dish, light and delicious, perfect for a vegan diet.

- 5 zucchini with the ends trimmed, sliced
- 1 large onion, peeled and cut julienne
- 6 garlic cloves, peeled and minced
- 3 tbsp. sunflower oil
- 1 tbsp. thyme, chopped
- 1 glass white dry wine (vegan and organic)
- 2 large tomatoes, peeled and cubed
- 1 bunch fresh dill, chopped
- Salt and pepper to taste

- ❖ In a deep skillet, preheat oil, then fry the zucchini over medium heat until golden. Cook in batches if necessary.
- ❖ Add the rest of the ingredients except dill. Cover with a lid. Reduce heat to the lowest possible setting and cook until zucchini are very tender for about 20 minutes.
- ❖ Serve hot, sprinkled with fresh dill.

Stews are great comfort food. This particular one is delicious served with a fresh cucumber salad or with summer peasant's salad.

67.   Stuffed Zucchini

This is a very simple recipe, adapted for the vegan diet. Vegetarians add a layer of cheese on top of the stuffing, usually caşcaval.

- 5 medium-size zucchini, halved
- 2 large onions, peeled and chopped
- 4 garlic cloves, peeled and minced
- 3 tbsp. sunflower oil
- 1 tbsp. mixed fresh herbs: thyme, oregano, dill
- 1 bunch fresh parsley, chopped
- Salt and pepper to taste

- ❖ Preheat oven to 175°C (350°F).
- ❖ Scoop out the seeds and the flesh of the zucchini and place in a deep bowl. Add the rest of the ingredients except parsley and mix well.
- ❖ Preheat a deep non-stick skillet over medium heat, then pour in the mixture and sauté for 10 minutes until the onion becomes translucent.
- ❖ Use the mixture to fill in the zucchini, then place them on a baking tray covered with parchment paper. Bake for 40 minutes.
- ❖ Serve hot, decorated with fresh parsley.

This dish goes nicely with rice and salad. Optionally, you can add a splash of olive oil over each zucchini half before serving and decorate with fresh cherry tomatoes.

68.   Stuffed Peppers

Remember that this is a traditional Romanian specialty that can be cooked either as a main dish with tomato sauce, or as ciorbă – recipe 55 in the previous chapter.

For the stuffed peppers:

- 6-8 bell peppers
- 2 leeks, washed, trimmed and minced
- 4-5 carrots, grated
- 100 g rice
- 2 tbsp. yellow maize flour
- 500 g mushrooms, minced
- 1 tbsp. fresh dill
- 1 tbsp. fresh parsley
- Salt and pepper to taste

For the sauce:

- 5 large tomatoes, peeled and cubed
- 200 ml tomato juice
- 1 red onion, peeled and minced
- 6-8 garlic cloves, peeled and minced
- 1 tbsp. sweet paprika powder
- 1 tsp. honey
- 1 tbsp. fresh garden herbs chopped: thyme, oregano
- 3 tbsp. oil
- Salt and pepper to taste

- To make the sauce, preheat oil in a deep skillet over medium heat. Sauté the onions for about 10 minutes.
- Add garlic and sweet paprika. Allow to cook, stirring frequently, for 3-5 minutes.
- Tip in the tomatoes. Add the tomato juice. Cook for about 30 minutes, until the sauce gets a creamy texture.
- Season with herbs, honey, salt and pepper to taste. Remove from heat.
- Preheat the oven to 200°C (400°F).
- Prepare your bell peppers. Cut a thin slice from the stem end of each bell pepper to remove the top. Carefully remove the seeds and the membranes and rinse well. Return to the mixture of mushrooms and rice. Add dill, parsley, maize flour, salt and pepper and mix well.
- Stuff peppers with the mixture, but leave a small space at the top since the rice will continue to expand. Place the peppers inside a deep, non-stick baking tray in a vertical position.
- Pour the tomato sauce over the peppers and insert the tray into the oven. Cook for 15-20 minutes. Serve hot with rice and salad.

69.   Roasted Peppers Stew

To learn how to roast peppers, refer to recipe 27 from the first chapter of the book.

- 7-10 whole red sweet banana peppers
- 5 large tomatoes, peeled and cubed
- 200 ml water
- 2 large onions, peeled and minced
- 8 garlic cloves, peeled and minced
- 3 tbsp. sunflower oil
- 1 bunch fresh dill, chopped
- Salt and pepper to taste

- ❖ Roast the peppers. Clean them carefully and cut them in long stripes.
- ❖ Preheat a deep non-stick skillet over medium heat. Sauté the onion in oil for 10 minutes, stirring frequently.
- ❖ Add garlic, water and tomatoes. Allow to cook for 15 minutes, before adding the peppers.
- ❖ Cover with a lid and reduce heat to minimum possible level. Cook 30 minutes, stirring gently from time to time. Be careful not to damage the peppers.
- ❖ Season with salt and pepper to taste. Add the dill. Stir gently and remove from heat.

Serve hot with rice or polenta. The dish is also good cold, on toast, on pita, or on fresh homemade bread.

70.   Potato and Peppers Stew

Potatoes are a staple of the Romanian cuisine, extremely versatile and present in many traditional dishes. They taste amazing in combination with other vegetables. This is one of my favorite childhood summer recipes. It's easy to make in the winter too if you use canned tomatoes and frozen peppers.

- 8 large potatoes, peeled and cubed
- 8 bell peppers, trimmed, deseeded and cubed
- 5 large tomatoes, peeled and cubed
- 200 ml water or vegetable stock
- 1 red onion, peeled and minced
- 6 garlic cloves, peeled and minced
- 3 tbsp. sunflower oil
- Salt and pepper to taste

- ❖ Preheat a deep non-stick skillet over medium heat. Sauté the onion in oil for 10 minutes, stirring frequently.
- ❖ Add garlic and allow to cook together with the onion, stirring frequently, for about 3 more minutes.
- ❖ Tip in the peppers, cover with a lid, and cook for 10 more minutes. Stir from time to time, until the peppers are slightly softened.
- ❖ Add water, tomatoes and potatoes. Reduce heat to the minimum level. Cover and cook for 1 hour.
- ❖ Season with salt and pepper to taste. Remove from heat.

Serve hot with polenta, or with toast and fresh seasonal salad. Serving with rice is an option, however not traditional.

71.   Potato Stew with Dill and Garlic

Easier to make than any other potato-based stew, this dish requires a few basic ingredients and can be made in every season. In the winter, use frozen dill instead of dried.

- 8 large potatoes, peeled and cubed
- 2 large onions, peeled and minced
- 200 ml water or vegetable stock

- 10 garlic cloves, peeled and minced
- 1 bunch fresh dill, chopped
- 3 tbsp. sunflower oil
- Salt and pepper to taste

- ❖ Preheat a deep non-stick skillet over medium heat. Sauté the onion in oil for 10 minutes, stirring frequently.
- ❖ Add ¾ of the garlic and allow to cook together with the onion, stirring frequently for about 3 more minutes.
- ❖ Add water and potatoes. Reduce heat to the minimum level. Cover and cook for 1 hour before adding the rest of the garlic, and salt and pepper to taste.
- ❖ Remove from heat, sprinkle with dill, and serve.

Serve hot with a fresh seasonal salad. The dish doesn't need a side dish. Due to its rich garlic content and taste, it goes well with polenta.

72.   Simple Potato Stew

Another easy potato-based stew, this dish is aromatic and light, perfect for every season.

- 8 large potatoes, peeled and cubed
- 1 large onion, peeled and minced
- 1 large carrot, grated
- 1 large bell pepper, trimmed, deseeded and cut into strips,
- 200 ml water or vegetable stock
- 1 tbsp. dried oregano

- 1 tbsp. sweet paprika powder
- 2 tbsp. tomato paste
- 1 bunch fresh parsley (or 2-3 tbsp. frozen parsley in the winter)
- 3 tbsp. sunflower oil
- Salt and pepper to taste

- ❖ Preheat a deep non-stick skillet over medium heat. Sauté the onion with the dried oregano and sweet paprika powder in oil for 10 minutes, stirring frequently.
- ❖ Add tomato paste and stir. Cook for 3 more minutes before adding the water, potato, carrot and bell pepper.
- ❖ Reduce heat to minimum, cover and cook for 1 hour, before seasoning with salt and pepper to taste.
- ❖ Remove from heat and mix in the parsley.

Serve hot, with bread and a fresh seasonal salad.

73.   Potato and Vegetables Stew

This is a traditional recipe with many variations all over the country. You can put pretty much everything you want into it.

- 4 large potatoes, peeled and cubed
- 200 grams green beans (string beans or snap beans)
- 1 large onion, peeled and minced
- 1 large carrot, cubed
- 2 large tomatoes, peeled and cubed
- 1 large bell pepper, trimmed, deseeded and cubed
- 1 zucchini, trimmed and cubed,
- 300 ml water or vegetable stock
- 1 tbsp. sweet paprika powder
- 1 bunch fresh parsley and dill, chopped
- 3 tbsp. sunflower oil
- Salt and pepper to taste

- ❖ Preheat a deep non-stick skillet over medium heat. Sauté the onion with the sweet paprika powder in oil for 10 minutes, stirring frequently.
- ❖ Add all the ingredients, except parsley, dill, salt and pepper. Cover and reduce heat to minimum. Cook for 1 hour – until the potatoes are done – , before seasoning with salt and pepper to taste.
- ❖ Remove from heat and mix in the parsley and dill.

Serve hot with bread and a fresh seasonal salad.

74.   Peas and Shallots Stew

If you like peas, you will love this dish. It is beautifully green. It is traditionally cooked with succulent, fresh green peas. If you cannot find them at the farmers' markets in season, you can also use frozen green peas for this recipe.

- 1 kg fresh green peas
- 150 grams shallots, peeled and minced
- 2 heads loose-leaf lettuce, washed and coarsely chopped
- 2 large potatoes, peeled and cubed
- 400 ml water or vegetable stock

- 1 bunch fresh parsley, chopped
- 1 bunch fresh dill, chopped
- 3 tbsp. sunflower oil
- Salt and pepper to taste

- ❖ Preheat a deep non-stick skillet over medium heat. Sauté the shallots in oil for 10 minutes, stirring frequently.
- ❖ Add the potatoes and water. Cook for 25 minutes, or until the potatoes are done (they should be easily pierced with a fork).
- ❖ Add the peas and the salad. Season with salt and pepper to taste. Continue boiling until the peas are done – about 5 minutes (they should be tender, yet crispy and green).
- ❖ Season with salt and pepper to taste. Mix in the parsley and dill before removing from heat.

Serve hot with bread and fresh tomato salad.

75.   Simple Peas Stew

Not as interesting as the peas and shallots stew, this recipe is nevertheless a good example of a traditional dish based on fresh green peas. In the absence of fresh peas, you can use canned or frozen.

- 1 kg fresh green peas
- 2 carrots, grated
- 1 onion, peeled and minced
- 3 tbsp. tomato paste
- 400 ml water or vegetable stock

- 1 bunch fresh dill, chopped
- 3 tbsp. sunflower oil
- 1 tsp. vinegar
- Salt and pepper to taste

❖ Preheat a deep non-stick skillet over medium heat. Sauté the onion with tomato paste in oil for 10 minutes, stirring frequently.

❖ Add the carrots. Cover with half of the water. Cook for 15 minutes before adding the peas and vinegar.

❖ Pour the rest of the water and simmer for 20 minutes before seasoning with salt and pepper to taste.

❖ Mix in the dill. Continue cooking for 2 more minutes. Remove from heat.

Please keep in mind that, while some recipes ask to cook peas less than 7 minutes to preserve their color and crunchy texture, this particular recipe calls for a longer cooking time. The vinegar keeps your green peas crispy, despite the khaki green color. Serve hot with bread and fresh tomato salad.

76.   Peas with Mushrooms and Vegetables Stew

Not as interesting as the peas and shallots stew, this recipe is nevertheless a good example of a traditional dish based on fresh green peas. In the absence of fresh peas, you can use canned or frozen.

- ½ kg fresh green peas
- ½ kg fresh mushrooms (white champignons)
- 1 carrot, thinly sliced crosswise
- 2 onions, peeled and minced
- 2 garlic cloves, peeled and minced
- 1 bell pepper, trimmed, deseeded and cubed

- 2 large tomatoes, peeled and cubed
- 1 tbsp. tomato paste
- 1 tbsp. sweet paprika powder
- 1 bunch fresh dill, chopped
- 3 tbsp. sunflower oil
- 1 tsp. vinegar
- 400 ml water
- Salt and pepper to taste

- ❖ Preheat a deep non-stick skillet over medium heat. Sauté the onion with tomato paste and paprika powder in oil for 10 minutes, stirring frequently.
- ❖ Add all the ingredients except the dill and the salt and pepper. Cover with a lid. Reduce to low heat and simmer for 30 minutes, stirring occasionally.
- ❖ Mix in the dill. Season with salt and pepper. Continue cooking for 2 more minutes before removing from heat.

Serve hot with bread and fresh seasonal salad.

77.   Monks' Vegetable Stew

The title of this dish is self-explanatory. You will find this traditional specialty, with variations, in many Romanian monasteries and even in restaurants and homes. Many Romanians consider it an art to get this stew right, but to be honest… there's nothing really complicated about it. Just prepare to have a large number of ingredients. At least use the ones in this base recipe:

- 2 large carrots, sliced crosswise (thinly)
- 1 large onion, peeled and cut julienne
- 2 large potatoes, peeled and cubed
- ½ celeriac, peeled and cubed
- 200 grams fresh green peas
- 200 grams snap beans
- 2 zucchinis, cubed
- 3 large tomatoes, peeled and cubed
- ¼ cabbage, hard core removed and cut julienne
- 1 large eggplant, cubed
- ½ cauliflower head coarsely chopped
- 100 ml oil
- 50 ml dry white wine
- 5-6 garlic cloves, peeled and minced
- 400 ml water
- 1 bunch fresh parsley, chopped
- 1 bunch fresh dill, chopped
- Salt and pepper to taste

- ❖ Preheat the oven to 180°C (355°F).
- ❖ Place a non-stick, over-friendly skillet over medium heat. Sauté the onion together with the carrots, celeriac, cauliflower, cabbage, and potatoes in oil for about 10 minutes, stirring frequently (but gently). Ladle in the water and cook for 10 minutes until the potatoes are almost done.
- ❖ Add ½ of the tomatoes, cabbage, zucchini, bell peppers, eggplant and garlic. and continue simmering for about 15 more minutes before adding the rest of the tomatoes, fresh green peas, and snap beans. Continue simmering for about 5 minutes before adding the wine.
- ❖ Season with salt and pepper to taste. Allow to simmer for 5 more minutes, until the alcohol has evaporated and all the flavors are well incorporated.
- ❖ Insert the skillet into the preheated oven. Allow to cook for 20 more minutes. Stir in the dill and parsley and serve hot.

78.   Mushrooms Ciulama

Ciulama is a dish that originates in the Turkish cuisine, however, Romanians have adapted it to their own lifestyle and needs. The non-vegan variant of the dish is made with chicken meat, while the vegan and vegetarian option is made with mushrooms. Ciulama is traditionally served with mămăligă (polenta), but you can always enjoy it with bread.

- 500 grams fresh mushrooms (large champignons)
- 1 onion, peeled and halved
- 2 carrots, whole
- 1 whole parsnip, peeled
- 3 l water

- 1 bunch fresh parsley, chopped (optional)
- 3 tbsp. flour
- 3 tbsp. oil
- Salt and pepper to taste

- ❖ Clean the mushrooms. Wash and boil in 1.5 l salted water for 15 minutes, then drain.
- ❖ In a deep soup pot add the rest of the water and salt to taste. Then add the boiled mushrooms, carrots, and parsnip. Cook over medium heat until all the veggies are nice and soft, for about 35 minutes.
- ❖ Remove from heat, drain, but keep the broth. Remove onion, carrots and parsnip. Do not discard them (a serving tip follows below this recipe).
- ❖ In a non-stick skillet – preheated – brown the flour in oil over medium heat stirring constantly for about 4 minutes, until it turns to a bright yellow.
- ❖ Ladle in the strained broth and continue stirring vigorously to avoid lumping.
- ❖ Once you have all the broth in, tip in the mushrooms and continue cooking for about 10 minutes, until the sauce becomes as consistent as a thick sour cream.
- ❖ Season with salt and pepper to taste, then remove from heat and sprinkle with fresh parsley (optional).

Remember to stir your ciulama as often as possible. Flour has a tendency to stick, regardless the type of the pan you use.

Ciulama is traditionally served with polenta, but it tastes equally delicious with fresh bread. A nice lettuce salad or pickles work wonders as a side dish.

79.   Plachie (Ragout) of Leeks with Tomato Paste

Plachie is usually a fish dish. Since there is no official English translation of this term, suffice is to say that it may also refer to a dish based on onion and cooked inside an oven. The exception is a "plachie of rice," which is a sweet dish. The term is based on the Greek "plaki," which is traditionally a fish-based dish. However, Romanian cuisine has adapted the original recipe to its own traditions. Therefore, you often find vegetable-based "plachie" in many Romanian homes and restaurants.

- 1 kg fresh leeks, properly cleaned and cut into thin slices
- 2 large onions, peeled and minced
- 3 tbsp. tomato paste
- 100 ml oil
- 5-6 garlic cloves, peeled and minced
- 200 ml water
- 1 bunch fresh parsley, chopped
- Salt and pepper to taste

- ❖ Preheat the oven to 180°C (355°F).
- ❖ Place a non-stick skillet over medium heat. Sauté the onion with the leeks in oil for about 15 minutes, stirring frequently.
- ❖ Add the tomato paste and water. Season with salt and pepper to taste. Allow everything to simmer for about 10 more minutes.
- ❖ Pour mixture into a baking dish and place into the oven to cook for 20 minutes.
- ❖ Take the baking dish out of the oven, then stir in the parsley and garlic. Return to the oven and continue cooking for 20 more minutes.

Serve hot with boiled potatoes or with polenta. The dish tastes nice cold too, when you can enjoy it on toast or on fresh pita bread.

80.   Plachie (Ragout) of White Beans with Red Peppers

The "plachie" principle described in the previous recipe applies to this dish too. You need boiled beans for it, or canned white beans. Traditionally, it is made with leftover beans (beans boiled the previous day for a different recipe), but you can also make it fresh (which is my preferred method).

- 1 cup dry beans (soaked for about 6 hours)
- 2 large onions, peeled and cut julienne
- 2 bell peppers (preferably red), trimmed, deseeded and minced
- 250 ml tomato juice
- 100 ml oil
- 50 ml dry white wine
- 5 garlic cloves, peeled and minced·
- 1 tsp. freshly chopped oregano
- 1 heaped tbsp. freshly chopped dill
- 1 heaped tbsp. freshly chopped parsley
- 2 dried bay leaves
- Salt and pepper to taste

- ❖ Preheat the oven to 180°C (355°F).
- ❖ In a large pot place one part beans and three parts water. Add the bay leaves, then bring gently to boil. Cook until the beans are nice and soft (for about 1 hour, but it could take longer, depending on the variety of beans that you used. Romanians use typically Phaseolus vulgaris, the common bean.).
- ❖ While the beans are boiling place a non-stick skillet over medium heat. Sauté the onion with salt and pepper to taste for about 10 minutes, stirring frequently until the onion becomes translucent.
- ❖ Pour the wine over the beans. Continue simmering for 5 minutes to allow the alcohol to evaporate.
- ❖ Add tomato juice and herbs. Cook for 5 more minutes. The sauce is now done.
- ❖ When the beans are boiled, pour them into a deep baking ramekin. Add the sauce and the garlic. Stir gently to incorporate the ingredients well.
- ❖ Place the ramekin into the preheated oven. Cook for 10 to 15 minutes, until the oil raises at the surface.

81.   Iahnie of White Beans

The "plachie" principle described in the previous recipe applies to this dish too. You need boiled beans for it, or canned white beans. Traditionally, it is made with leftover beans (beans boiled the previous day for a different recipe), but you can also make it fresh (which is my preferred method).

- 300 grams dry beans (soaked for about 6 hours)
- 1 large onion, peeled and quartered
- 2 large carrots, halved
- 4 large onions, peeled and cut minced
- 100 ml oil
- 6 garlic cloves, peeled and minced
- 1 sprig oregano, or 1 bay leaf
- 1 heaped tbsp. freshly chopped parsley
- 1 tbsp. sweet paprika powder
- 1 tbsp. tomato paste
- Salt and pepper to taste

- ❖ Bring the beans to a boil, allow to scald for 3-4 minutes, then drain.
- ❖ Put the beans in a large pot with fresh water. Add the quartered onion, the oregano and the carrots. Boil until the beans are tender – about 1 hour. Drain. You can keep or discard the vegetables – it's up to your personal preference.
- ❖ In a deep non-stick skillet, sauté the minced onion until golden, then add the sweet paprika and the tomato paste.
- ❖ Cook for 5 more minutes, stirring frequently, before adding the beans.
- ❖ Season with salt and pepper to taste. Cook for 10 more minutes, stirring occasionally.
- ❖ Mix in the parsley and remove from heat.

Serve hot, with fresh bread and pickles.

82.   Braised Cabbage (Varză Dulce Călită)

This is one of those special, traditional dishes considered a staple in many Romanian households all over the country. Like most traditional recipes, the ingredients and methods of preparation vary, depending on each home. Traditionally, you find meat and fat (like bacon) in varză călită, but vegan options exist and they are equally interesting.

- 1 large cabbage, hard core removed, leaves cut julienne
- 1 spicy red pepper, minced – or ½ tsp. spicy paprika powder (or more, if you like spicy foods)
- ½ l homemade tomato juice
- 3 tbsp. sunflower oil
- 1 tbsp. salt
- 1 tbsp. citric acid crystalline powder
- 1 string oregano
- 1 bay leaf
- 1 bunch fresh dill, chopped

- ❖ Sprinkle salt and citric acid crystalline powder all over the cabbage (remember, it has to be already cut julienne) and massage it well with your hands until the vegetable begins to sweat, releasing its juice. Set aside.
- ❖ In a deep non-stick skillet, preheat oil over high heat. Toss in the cabbage once the oil is hot. Toss a few times for about 2 minutes, then reduce heat to medium.
- ❖ Allow to cook for 5 minutes, then add the tomato juice and the spicy pepper or spicy paprika powder. Mix well. Add the oregano and the bay leaf. Cover with a lid and reduce heat to medium.
- ❖ Allow the cabbage to cook for 30 minutes, until the leaves are nice and soft. Stir occasionally to help the flavors blend well.
- ❖ Remove from heat, remove the oregano and the bay leaf, and mix in the dill.

Serve hot with polenta.

83.   Braised Sauerkraut (Varză Acră Călită)

The winter equivalent of the previous dish, the recipe for vegan varză acră călită is pretty similar, too. You can make this dish in the summer too if you have sauerkraut. Refer to recipe 30 in this book to find out how to make traditional Romanian sauerkraut. Remember, the full health benefits of sauerkraut are only derived from the raw product. While cooked sauerkraut may retain some of the benefits, this dish is not as healthy as it is tasty.

- 800 grams sauerkraut
- 2 large onions, peeled and cut julienne
- 3 tbsp. sunflower oil
- 3 tbsp. tomato paste
- 1 tbsp. dried oregano
- 1 tbsp. sweet paprika powder
- 300 ml water
- 1 tsp. whole peppercorns

- ❖ In a deep non-stick skillet, sauté onion with tomato paste, dried oregano, and paprika powder for about 10 minutes, stirring frequently.
- ❖ Toss in the sauerkraut, add water and peppercorns, then reduce heat to medium.
- ❖ Allow the sauerkraut to cook for about 50 minutes, until it gets a beautiful color and it softens. Remember to stir occasionally.

Serve hot with polenta. If you cook this in the summer, replace the tomato paste with 4 large fresh tomatoes, skinned and cubed. If you don't have tomato paste in the winter, you can always use 1 small can of peeled tomatoes.

84. Vegan Sarmale (Stuffed Cabbage)

Sarmale, the beloved, national Romanian dish, is traditionally a meat-based main dish enjoyed at special occasions, such as Christmas and weddings. Yes, it's a special type of main dish, because it takes ages to prepare. Making sarmale is the true test of cookery skill. Vegan sarmale is even trickier because you need to get the filling just right. You can always make sarmale with regular cabbage leaves, but it is better with pickled cabbage (and that's the real, traditional way to prepare it).

- 1 pickled cabbage head
- ½ kg mushrooms (champignons), minced
- 2 large onions, peeled and finely minced
- 2 carrots, grated
- 1 celeriac head, peeled and grated
- 4 large tomatoes, peeled and cubed

- 200 grams white rice, washed, but uncooked
- 3 tbsp. sunflower oil
- 1 tbsp. dried oregano
- 1 tbsp. sweet paprika powder
- ½ homemade tomato juice
- Ground pepper to taste

❖ In a deep non-stick skillet, sauté onion with dried oregano and paprika powder for about 10 minutes over medium heat, stirring frequently.

❖ Add carrots, celeriac, and mushrooms. Continue cooking and stirring until the root vegetables are nice and soft.

❖ Add the mushrooms. Allow to cook for about 10 more minutes. Remove from heat. Mix in the uncooked rice. Season with pepper to taste and set aside.

❖ Prepare your pickled cabbage. Remove the leaves from the cabbage one by one. Be careful not to tear them up. Cut the hard nervures (cores) and set them aside. Place the prepared leaves carefully on a plate to have them ready for filling with the mushroom mixture. If the leaves are too big, cut them in half. Keep 2 or 3 leaves whole, you will need them to cover the sarmale.

❖ Chop the cores of the cabbage and line the bottom of a deep, non-stick, oven-friendly pot with them.

❖ Working carefully, leaf by leaf, roll a spoonful of mushroom mixture into the cabbage leaves. Fold the right side in, then roll up from the stem end. Press the left end in. This holds the entire roll together (it will look like a small stuffed envelope). The size of the roll is a matter of personal preference. Just try to get them approximately the same size.

❖ After you finish rolling all the mushroom mixture into cabbage leaves, place your sarmale in the deep pot that you have previously lined up with the chopped thick core stems of the cabbage. Make a circle of sorts and try to leave the center empty. You can layer the sarmale on top of each other.

- ❖ Place the cubed tomatoes in the center of the pot, then pour the tomato juice over the contents of the pot. If all the sarmale are not fully covered, complete with cold water.
- ❖ Cover the sarmale with 2 or 3 whole pickled cabbage leaves to make a lid of sorts. Boil over very low heat. When the sarmale begin boiling (it takes a while) shake the pot a little, carefully, to make sure nothing sticks to the bottom. Repeat this from time to time – every 15 minutes or so.
- ❖ Depending on the size of your pot and on the thickness of the cabbage, it can take as many as 4 hours to cook this dish. The sarmale are ready when the cabbage is soft and breaks easily when cut with a fork. You can try the loose leaves on top before ending the cooking time.

Serve hot with polenta. The methods for cooking this dish vary depending on region and household. Each home in Romania has its own recipe. While some people prefer to cook the sarmale slowly on the stove, others bake them in the oven. Others begin the cooking process on the stove and end it in the oven. It's all up to you. In the end, sarmale taste delicious, regardless their size or the manner in which they were cooked.

85. Vegan Cabbage "a la Cluj"

As the title of this dish suggests, this is a recipe traditional in the Romanian city of Cluj, in Transylvania. A variant of this is "Sauerkraut a la Cluj." It is the same recipe, but you replace the cabbage head with 1 kg sauerkraut.

- 1 head of cabbage (about 1kg) hard core removed and cut julienne
- 2 onions, peeled and minced
- 100 grams rice
- 100 grams fresh mushrooms, minced
- 50 grams raisins
- 4 large tomatoes, peeled and cubed (or a can of tomatoes)
- 100 ml sunflower oil
- 1 bunch fresh dill, chopped
- 2 tbsp. fresh or 1 tbsp. dry oregano
- 1 tbsp. sweet paprika powder
- Salt and pepper to taste

❖ Rub the cabbage with salt and set aside to breathe for 15 minutes. It will release its juices and you have to drain it well by squeezing the cabbage with your hands.
❖ Squeeze the juice from the mushrooms too.
❖ In the meantime, cook the rice with the raisins.
❖ Drain the juice of the tomatoes into a bowl. Split the flesh in two equal parts.
❖ Sauté the onion in oil with sweet paprika powder over medium heat for 4-5 minutes. Add the mushrooms. Simmer until the juice evaporates. Remove from heat, mix in the rice and set aside.
❖ Preheat the oven to 175°C (345°F).
❖ In a deep skillet sauté the cabbage in oil and sweet paprika powder for 15-20 minutes, stirring occasionally. Add the oregano and the dill and mix well.
❖ Layer a clay or a ceramic baking tray with ½ the quantity of cabbage, then layer the mushrooms and rice mixture. Finally, add a layer with the rest of the cabbage. Finish with the rest of the tomatoes and tomato juice. Season with salt and pepper.
❖ Bake in the oven for 50 to 60 minutes, until all the liquids evaporate and the top of the cabbage is crisp (but not burned).

"Gulaș" is the Romanian alternative to a beloved iconic Hungarian dish. This is a recipe adapted from an original from the Prislop Monastery in Hunedoara, Transylvania. Traditionally, gulaș is made over an open wood fire, in a special cauldron.

- 800 grams mixed mushrooms (wild and champignons), cleaned and chopped coarsely
- 1 onion, peeled and minced
- 4 garlic cloves, peeled and minced
- 2 red banana peppers, trimmed, deseeded and chopped coarsely
- 2 potatoes, peeled and cubed
- 4 tomatoes, peeled and cubed
- 6 tbsp. sunflower oil (or any other cooking oil you want)
- 1 tbsp. sweet paprika powder
- 1 tbsp. vinegar
- 1 tbsp. maple syrup (instead of sugar)
- 2 bay leaves
- 1 tbsp. fresh oregano
- 2-3 sprigs rosemary
- 1 bunch fresh parsley, chopped
- Salt and pepper to taste
- 400 ml hot water

- ❖ In a deep pot sauté onion, banana peppers and paprika powder in oil over medium heat, stirring occasionally, for about 8 minutes. Add the garlic and continue cooking for 3-4 minutes before adding the mushrooms.
- ❖ Reduce heat to low. Cook for 25 minutes, stirring occasionally, before adding the tomatoes, bay leaves and 200 ml hot water.
- ❖ Allow the mixture to simmer for about 10 minutes before adding the rest of the spices. Season with vinegar, maple syrup, salt and pepper to taste. Tip in the potatoes, oregano and rosemary. Stir and make sure that the potatoes are entirely covered with the sauce. Complete with water as needed.
- ❖ Cook until the potatoes are done, then remove from heat. Remove the bay leaves and the rosemary sprigs. Sprinkle with parsley. Serve hot.

87. Dill Stew

This is one of those dishes that will surprise you if you enjoy strong flavors. It is an unlikely use for dill, but the taste is amazing.

- 350 grams dill (about 2 large bunches), coarsely chopped
- 3 onions, peeled and minced
- 1 leek (only the white part), finely chopped
- 3 garlic cloves, peeled and minced
- 1 large carrot, grated
- 1 bell pepper, trimmed, deseeded and finely cubed
- 2 large tomatoes, peeled and cubed
- 4 tbsp. oil
- 1 tbsp. flour
- 400 ml cold water (or vegetable stock)
- Salt and pepper to taste

❖ In a deep pot sauté onion, leek, bell pepper and carrot in oil over medium heat for about 10 minutes until the onion softens.

❖ Add the tomatoes and reduce the heat to low. Cover with a lid and allow to simmer for 10 minutes. Stir occasionally.

❖ Dissolve the flour in water or stock and pour it in the pot. Add the dill and mix well.

❖ Allow to simmer for about 10 minutes, until the dill is nice and soft, then add the garlic and season with salt and pepper.

❖ Remove from heat. Set aside 5 minutes before serving.

Serve on toast, as is, or as a side dish for stuffed zucchini (recipe 67), stuffed peppers (recipe 68), boiled or baked potatoes, or stuffed eggplant. The dill stew can also be enjoyed cold. It tends to taste better the next day, as the flavours have a chance to set.

88.   Dill and Mushrooms Stew

Another dill-based recipe that adds a lot of flavor to your plate is dill and mushrooms stew. It is not a variation of the previous recipe.

- 1 kg fresh mushrooms (white champignons), cleaned and coarsely chopped
- 1 large onion, peeled and minced
- 6 garlic cloves, peeled and minced
- 2 tbsp. tomato paste
- 4 tbsp. oil
- 100 ml hot water (or vegetable stock)
- 2 large bunches dill, coarsely chopped
- Salt and pepper to taste

- ❖ In a deep pot, sauté onion in oil over medium heat for about 10 minutes, until golden.
- ❖ Add garlic, water and the tomato paste. Mix well.
- ❖ Tip in the mushrooms. Cover with a lid. Reduce heat (close to low, but not the lowest temperature). Simmer for 20 minutes.
- ❖ Add the dill and season the stew with salt and pepper to taste. Cover with the lid. Reduce heat to the absolute lowest temperature and simmer for 20 more minutes, stirring occasionally.
- ❖ Remove from heat. Set aside 5 minutes before serving.

Serve warm with pita, toast or polenta. You can also enjoy this dish with a side of boiled or baked potatoes.

89. Cauldron Fried New Potatoes with Garlic and Dill

This traditional recipe counts on very fresh, bite-sized potatoes (also known as baby potatoes). You don't necessarily need a cauldron – a very deep cooking pot with a thick bottom will do. It is a spring/early summer dish, popular in many regions of the country. International variations exist, but they replace dill with rosemary and use less oil (also the potatoes are boiled before pan-frying or pan-roasting).

- ½ kg petite potatoes, washed (skins on) and dried
- Frying oil
- 2-3 green garlics, finely chopped
- 1 bunch fresh dill, coarsely chopped
- Salt to taste

- ❖ In a deep pot, preheat the oil over medium heat.
- ❖ Add the potatoes, making sure that the oil almost covers them.
- ❖ Cover the pot with a lid. Fry for about 25-30 minutes, stirring occasionally with a spatula to ensure that the potatoes fry evenly on all sides.
- ❖ When the potatoes are almost ready tip in the garlic. Allow to fry for 1 more minute.
- ❖ Remove from heat. Carefully take the potatoes out with a spatula.
- ❖ Set the potatoes in a salad bowl (without drying off the fat with kitchen towels). Season with salt and mix in the dill.

Serve hot with a light salad or pickles.

90. Stuffed Eggplant

This recipe is derived from Turkish cuisine and is traditional in the south of Romania, although it can be found in several variations in many other regions. Eggplants are a staple in vegan and vegetarian cuisine and are favored in Romanian cuisine too.

- 2 large eggplants
- 1 large tomato, peeled and cubed
- 1 large onion, peeled and minced
- 4-6 garlic cloves, peeled and minced
- 3 tbsp. oil
- 1 bunch fresh parsley, chopped
- Sea salt to taste

❖ Preheat oven to 180°C (350°F).

❖ Cut the eggplants in halves lengthwise and scoop out the pulp, leaving enough inside the skin to hold its shape when baked. Rub the inside of the eggplants with sea salt and oil.

❖ Chop the scooped pulp in small cubes (preferably the size of a dice, but they can be a bit larger).

❖ In a skillet sauté onion and garlic in oil over medium heat until the onion is soft and golden.

❖ Add the pulp of the eggplant, half of the parsley, and the tomato. Simmer, stirring occasionally, for 15 to 20 minutes.

❖ Place the eggplant halves on a baking tray covered with parchment paper.

❖ Scoop pulp and tomato mixture into each eggplant half, Place the tray into the oven to bake for 40-50 minutes – depending on the size of your eggplants.

❖ Remove from the oven and sprinkle with the rest of the parsley.

Serve warm with a light salad and a side of rice. You can also serve a side of dill stew with this main dish. Variations of stuffed eggplant may include mushrooms and bell peppers, which are sautéed with the tomato, eggplant pulp, onions and garlic to form the filling.

91. Eggplant with Tomato Sauce

Vegan and vegetarian, absolutely delicious, this is a recipe I hold very close to my heart. I was too young to remember who taught me how to make it. This tasty wonder has been in my family for generations.

- 3 fresh eggplants
- 5-6 fresh, medium-sized tomatoes, peeled and diced
- A bunch of fresh oregano and basil, finely chopped
- 5 garlic cloves, peeled and minced
- 4 shallots, peeled and minced
- 100 ml dry white wine
- 1 cup white flour (to dust the eggplants)
- Frying oil (sunflower traditionally, but you can use your favorite)
- 1 tsp. sweet paprika powder
- 1 tbsp. agave syrup, or anything else you want to use instead of sugar
- Salt and pepper to taste

- ❖ Remove the stem ends of the eggplants. Slice each eggplant in halves lengthwise, then each half into long slices as thick as your index finger.
- ❖ Bring salted water to a boil in a deep cooking pot. Scald the eggplant for 5-6 minutes. Remove from heat. Drain well through a sieve.
- ❖ Prepare some all-purpose white flour on a plate – season it with salt and pepper.
- ❖ Heat oil in a large sauté pan. Roll the eggplant slices through flour, then fry until golden brown on each side. Don't crowd your pan. Fry several batches if you need to. Drain on kitchen towels, then set aside to cool off.
- ❖ In a non-stick pan, sauté paprika powder, onion and garlic in oil over medium heat, stirring frequently, for 8-10 minutes.
- ❖ Add a glass of white wine and stir occasionally until the liquid has evaporated.
- ❖ Tip in the tomatoes. Season with salt, black pepper and a teaspoon of agave syrup. Let simmer, stirring occasionally, for 15-20 minutes.
- ❖ Add a teaspoon of finely chopped oregano and basil before you remove from heat.

Serve hot or cold with toast, fresh bread, or pita. You can also enjoy it with a side of rice.

92.   Potatoes Baked in Dying Embers

One of the easiest recipes of the Romanian cuisine, but a tradition all over the country, this is something perfect for those summer days when you fire up the grill or you make a bonfire and the embers are dying, but still burning hot. The ashes give the potatoes a special taste that cannot be achieved through other methods of cooking. You need large, thick-skinned potatoes.

- As many potatoes as you want to bake
- Salt

- Olive oil

- ❖ Wash the potatoes well. Dry them with a towel.
- ❖ Make nests in the embers and place the potatoes carefully in. Make sure that no burning coals are in direct contact with the potatoes. You do not need to wrap the potatoes in aluminum foil – you can, but this completely changes the taste.
- ❖ Cover the potatoes with a thick layer of embers. Allow them to bake, undisturbed, for 45-50 minutes. They are ready when they can be easily pierced with the knife or with a metal skewer.
- ❖ Remove from the embers, dust off the ashes, and serve.

Serve hot, seasoned with salt and sprinkled with olive oil. You can enjoy baked potatoes with all kinds of salads, sauces and as sides for your favorite stews. The skins are edible and taste delicious, but many people choose to remove them because of the contact with the ashes.

93. Potato Pudding

It's still a mystery why this dish is called a pudding, but that's the English translation for the Romanian Budincă. Never mind the name, this is an easy dish, original, and fun to make.

- 8 large potatoes, peeled and cubed
- 2 large onions, peeled and minced
- 100 ml oil
- 2 tbsp. all-purpose flour
- 4 garlic cloves, peeled and minced
- 2 tbsp. breadcrumbs
- Salt and pepper to taste

- ❖ Preheat the oven to 200°C (400°F).
- ❖ Bring salted water to a boil. Cook the potatoes with minced onion until the potatoes are soft enough for a mash.
- ❖ Mash the potatoes and onions close to a paste with a hand masher.
- ❖ Mix in oil, flour, and garlic. Season with salt and pepper to taste.
- ❖ Grease a loaf pan with oil and sprinkle it with breadcrumbs.
- ❖ Pour in the potato mash. Place in the oven to bake for about 25-30 minutes, until it forms a golden crust at the top.
- ❖ Remove from heat. Allow it to cool off for 8-10 minutes before you take it out of the pan.

Serve on a bed of lettuce salad, garnished with parsley or dill. You can also serve a slice of the pudding with a spread (like zacuscă).

94.   Iahnie of Potatoes

There are hundreds of potato-based dishes in Romania – this, however, is one of my favorites.

- 8 large potatoes, peeled and cubed
- 2 large onions, peeled and minced
- 2 tbsp. oil
- 4 large tomatoes, peeled and coarsely cubed
- 2 bay leaves
- 1 bunch fresh parsley, chopped
- 1 tbsp. tomato paste
- 400 ml hot water
- Salt and pepper to taste

- ❖ Dissolve the tomato paste into 400 ml hot water.
- ❖ Sauté the onion in oil over medium heat until golden (10 minutes).
- ❖ Add the potatoes and the water with tomato paste. Reduce heat to low.
- ❖ Simmer for 10 minutes before adding the tomatoes and the bay leaves.
- ❖ Simmer until the potatoes are soft, then season with salt and pepper to taste. Remove from heat.
- ❖ Mix in the fresh parsley and serve hot.

Serve hot with polenta and pickles, or with bread and seasonal salad.

95. Leeks with Olives

Although they do not grow in Romania, olives are an integral part of our cuisine. Leeks, on the other hand, grow in abundance, especially in the south. In Oltenia. Romanians enjoy eating them raw during the colder seasons. This traditional recipe is a winter special.

- 6 leeks, trimmed and sliced crosswise
- 200 ml homemade tomato juice
- 2 large tomatoes, peeled and cubed
- 100 grams black olives, without pits
- 50 ml dry white wine
- 3 tbsp. cooking olive oil
- 1 tbsp. maple syrup (instead of sugar)
- Salt and pepper to taste

- ❖ Scald the leeks in boiling water for about 10 minutes. Drain well.
- ❖ In a non-stick skillet preheat the oil, then add the leeks, cover with a lid and sauté until golden (about 10 minutes). Stir occasionally to ensure that the leeks cook well on all sides.
- ❖ Add the tomatoes, tomato juice, wine, olives, a tablespoon of maple syrup, and the wine. Season with salt and pepper to taste, mix well, and allow the food to simmer for 15 more minutes.
- ❖ Remove from heat and serve hot.

Serve hot with fresh bread or with polenta.

96.   Celeriac with Olives

Celeriac is a humble root vegetable, yet full of flavor and very interesting in a variety of soups and main dishes. However, it is rarely used as a base ingredient in Romanian cuisine. This recipe from Muntenia changes things:

- 3 large celeriac knobs, peeled and cubed
- 6 tomatoes, peeled and cubed
- 4 large onions, peeled and minced
- 100 grams black olives, without pits
- 3 tbsp. cooking oil
- 1 tbsp. maple syrup (instead of sugar)
- 1 bunch fresh dill, chopped
- 1 bunch fresh parsley, chopped
- Salt and pepper to taste

- ❖ Preheat oil over medium heat in a deep non-stick skillet.
- ❖ Sauté onions for about 10 minutes, stirring frequently.
- ❖ Add a ladle of water and tip in the celeriac. Cover with a lid and cook for about 20 minutes. Stir occasionally.
- ❖ Add the tomatoes and the olives, plus a tablespoon of maple syrup. Allow to cook, covered, for 10 more minutes.
- ❖ Season with salt and pepper to taste. Mix in the dill and parsley before removing from heat.

Serve hot with fresh bread or with polenta. The dish is also excellent with seasonal salad or with pickles. You can also cook this recipe with potatoes instead of celeriac.

97. Dobrogea-style Musaca

Traditionally a dish specific to countries of the former Ottoman Empire, the "musaca" has its own variations in Romania.

- 3 large tomatoes, trimmed and cubed
- 4 large potatoes, peeled and cut into thin slices
- 3 large onions, minced
- 1 bell pepper, trimmed, deseeded, and minced
- 3 large tomatoes, peeled and cubed
- 2 large tomatoes, cut into thin slices
- 1 bunch fresh dill, chopped
- 1 bunch fresh parsley, chopped
- 50 ml dry white wine,
- 3 tbsp. oil
- Breadcrumbs
- Salt and pepper to taste

- ❖ Preheat the oven at 200°C (395°F).
- ❖ In a deep non-stick skillet, sauté onions in oil over medium heat for about 10 minutes, stirring frequently.
- ❖ Add cubed tomatoes, eggplant, pepper, and wine. Season with salt and pepper. Cover with a lid. Allow the vegetables to cook for 10-15 minutes. Remove from heat. Mix in the dill and parsley and sprinkle with breadcrumbs.
- ❖ Grease a ceramic baking tray with oil, then place slices of the potatoes in an even layer. Pour some of the eggplant mixture on top of this layer and arrange evenly. Continue layering potato and eggplant mixture, alternating. The last layer should be a potato layer. Add the tomato slices on top of this layer.
- ❖ Bake in the preheated oven for 40-50 minutes until the potatoes are done. The dish should be crispy at the top. Let set for 30 minutes before serving.

Serve warm, sprinkled with fresh parsley. A seasonal salad may accompany this main dish.

Tomatoes are a staple of Romanian cuisine. This dish has Turkish origins and is popular in some villages in the south of Romania.

- 8 large tomatoes
- ½ kg fresh mushrooms (champignons), chopped
- 1 large onion, peeled and minced
- 1 tbsp. oil
- 1 heaped tbsp. rice
- 50 ml water
- 1 bunch fresh parsley, chopped
- Breadcrumbs (optional)
- Salt and pepper to taste

- ❖ Cut off the tops of the tomatoes and scoop out the seeds and flesh into a salad bowl. Set the tomatoes with the cavities down to allow the juice to drain well.
- ❖ Chop the flesh of the tomatoes finely and set aside.
- ❖ Preheat the oil in a non-stick pan over medium heat. Sauté the onion until it becomes translucent (8-10 minutes).
- ❖ Tip in the tomato flesh and the mushrooms, cover and simmer until the juice of the mushrooms evaporate. Stir occasionally.
- ❖ Add the rice and 50 ml water. Season with salt and pepper. Turn the heat to low and simmer until the rice is cooked.
- ❖ Remove from heat and set aside to cool down. If the mixture is too runny add some breadcrumbs to give it consistency, or cook longer. When it is cold, mix in the parsley.
- ❖ Preheat the oven to 200°C/400°F
- ❖ Stuff the tomatoes with the mushrooms.

99. Vegan Veggie Pilaf

The humble rice can taste so good when cooked creatively. I love this about Romanian cuisine.

- 150 grams rice
- 450 ml water
- 1 carrot, grated
- 1 parsley root, peeled and grated
- 1 bell pepper (any color) trimmed, deseeded and finely cut julienne
- 1 large onion, peeled and minced

- 4 tbsp. oil
- 1 heaped tbsp. fresh parsley, chopped, plus some to garnish
- Salt and pepper to taste

- ❖ Preheat the oven to 200°C/400°F.
- ❖ Boil the rice in water with the carrot, root parsley, and bell pepper. Season with salt and pepper to taste.
- ❖ In a frying pan, sauté the onion in oil over medium heat, stirring frequently, for about 10 minutes.
- ❖ When the rice and veggies are boiled, mix in the sautéed onion and all its juices. Pour everything into an oven-friendly ramekin (ceramic tray, or clay ramekin).
- ❖ Bake for 25-30 minutes until the rice becomes golden-crispy at the surface.
- ❖ Remove from heat and serve hot.

Serve as is (as a main dish) or as a side dish with stuffed peppers, stuffed eggplant, or stuffed tomatoes. For example, a nice, fresh, seasonal salad served with this dish does wonders.

100. Pickled Cucumbers Stew

As strange as it may sound to stew pickled cucumbers, this is what they do in Oltenia. This is a tasty, creative dish. It has both vegan and meat-based variations. The recipe varies from household to household.

- 10 pickled cucumbers (pickled in old-fashioned salt-water-dill brie), cubed
- 1 large onion, peeled and minced
- 1 large carrot, grated
- 1 tbsp. flour
- 1 tbsp. tomato paste
- 1 tsp. sweet paprika powder
- 2 tbsp. oil
- 1 bunch fresh parsley, chopped
- 1 tsp. oregano
- 1 bay leaf
- 200 ml water or vegetable stock
- Water
- Pinch of freshly ground pepper

- ❖ In a deep non-stick skillet sauté onion and carrot in oil over medium heat, stirring frequently, for 10 minutes.
- ❖ Add flour, tomato paste, oregano, and sweet paprika powder. Ladle in some water and continue cooking, stirring continuously for 5 minutes until you get a consistent cream.
- ❖ Add the pickled cucumbers. Cover with water and allow to simmer for about 40 minutes, until the cucumbers soften. Stir occasionally. If the sauce is too thick, add more water.
- ❖ Before removing from heat, mix in the parsley and finish with a pinch of freshly ground pepper.

This dish is very interesting and popular in the winter, when it can also be served as a side dish for potato-based main dishes.

Instead of Conclusion

There are many other interesting vegan foods to discover in Romania, but, for the purpose of an introduction into our traditional cuisine this collection only features 100, including some of our iconic and legendary specialties: mămăligă (porridge), iahnie (baked beans), plachie (ragout), sarmale (stuffed cabbage), stuffed peppers, and zacuscă (vegetable spread).

The recipes you find here are my own, but many were simplified to give you a base to work with. If you are familiar with Romanian cuisine, you will also notice that many are different from what you learned from your relatives and from other Romanian cookbooks. This is because traditional cuisine is mostly verbally preserved and each housewife has her own cooking style and different recipes.

Feel free to improve the recipes to suit your palate. For instance, you may want more herbs, some spicy chili flakes, sugar to sweeten the taste of the tomatoes, and so on.

You will also notice that many recipes call for tomato paste – feel free to use fresh tomatoes instead. Also remember that our cuisine counts a lot on onions and garlic – so have plenty in your household. Other must-haves include parsley, dill, and sweet paprika powder.

Last but not least, this collection does not include desserts, simply because I am trying to keep away from sugar. Romanian desserts tend to be very sweet and sugar-rich. Vegan desserts are rare, but not nonexistent: pancakes, doughnuts, sweet breads, pies, and so on. A baker is a better person to reveal their secrets to you.

So instead of ending this collection with a dessert, I am leaving you with a sauce – the traditional garlic "mujdei," which is an amazing addition to grilled foods.

101.   Garlic "Mujdei"

While this is not a main dish, it doesn't really fit into any category of foods. Call it a sauce if you will, and serve it with whatever you fancy. Traditionally, we eat it with meats, but since this is a vegan book consider this as a dipping sauce for vegan patties, baked potato, or grilled vegetables.

- 10 garlic cloves, peeled
- 1 tsp. salt
- 200 ml water or vegetable stock

- Pinch of freshly ground pepper

- ❖ Crush the garlic vigorously with a pestle in a mortar. Add salt and continue pressing until the garlic becomes creamy.
- ❖ Add the water slowly. Mix well.
- ❖ Finish with a pinch of freshly ground pepper.

There are many things you can do to improve this recipe. For instance, you can enhance it with a spoonful of sweet paprika powder and rub it in vigorously with the crushed garlic before you add the liquid. Or, you can use tomato juice instead of water and stock. Finally, some recipes call for a drizzle of oil. A favorite use for mujdei is with roasted red banana peppers (recipe 27) instead of a simple marinade.

Printed in Great Britain
by Amazon